Successor journal to *Theatre Quarterly* (1971–1981)
VOLUME X   NUMBER 37   FEBRUARY 1994

Editors
CLIVE BARKER
SIMON TRUSSLER

Contents

*New Theatre Quarterly is published in February, May, August, and November by Cambridge University Press, The Edinburgh
Building, Shaftesbury Road, Cambridge CB2 2RU, England*   ISBN 0 521 46656 3   ISSN 0266-464X

Editorial Enquiries
Great Robhurst, Woodchurch, Ashford, Kent TN26 3TB, England
Unsolicited manuscripts are considered for publication in *New Theatre Quarterly*. They should be sent to Simon Trussler at the above address, but unless accompanied by a stamped addressed envelope (UK stamp or international reply coupons) return cannot be guaranteed. Contributors are asked to follow the journal's house style as closely as possible.

Advertising Enquiries
Advertising enquiries should be sent to the Journals Promotion Department at Cambridge or to the American Branch of Cambridge University Press.

Subscriptions
New Theatre Quarterly (ISSN: 0266-464X) is published quarterly by Cambridge University Press, The Edinburgh Building, Shaftesbury Road, Cambridge CB2 2RU, and The Journals Department, 40 West 20th Street, New York, NY 10011-4211.

Four parts form a volume. The subscription price, which includes postage (excluding VAT), of Volume X, 1994, is £41.00 (US$73.00 in the USA, Canada and Mexico) for institutions, £24.00 (US$37.00) for individuals ordering direct from the publishers and certifying that the Journal is for their personal use. Single parts cost £11.00 (US$19.00 in the USA, Canada and Mexico) plus postage. EC subscribers (outside the UK) who are not registered for VAT should add VAT at their country's rate. VAT registered subscribers should provide their VAT registration number.

Japanese prices for institutions (including ASP delivery) are available from Kinokuniya Company Ltd., P.O. Box 55, Chitose, Tokyo.

Orders, which must be accompanied by payment, may be sent to a bookseller or to the publishers (in the USA, Canada and Mexico to the American Branch).

Copies of the Journal for subscribers in the USA, Canada and Mexico are sent by air to New York to arrive with minimum delay. Second class postage paid at New York, NY, and at additional mailing offices. POSTMASTER: send address changes in the USA, Canada and Mexico to *New Theatre Quarterly*, Cambridge University Press, The Journals Department, 40 West 20th Street, New York, NY 10011-4211.

Claims for missing issues will only be considered if made immediately on receipt of the following issue.

Typeset by Country Setting, Woodchurch, Ashford, Kent TN26 3TB, and printed and bound in Great Britain by the University Press, Cambridge.

Eric Bentley
interviewed by Charles Marowitz

From Half-Century to Millennium: the Theatre and the Electric Spectator

Well into his eighth decade, Eric Bentley now regards himself as primarily a playwright, having redefined the agenda of serious criticism during the early post-war years, pioneered the understanding, translation, and production of Brecht in the West, and for long combined academic work at Columbia with producing the best kind of regular theatre reviews. Apart from several collections of that 'occasional' writing, and anthologies of plays in translation which have helped to extend the range of the English-language repertoire, he has produced several full-length studies of seminal importance – from his early re-evaluation of Shaw and, in *The Playwright as Thinker*, of other major modern dramatists, to the more theoretical but invariably stimulating 'rethink' of dramatic genres in *The Life of the Drama*. More recently, he has devoted his time to active playwriting, and it was during a production of his *Lord Alfred's Lover* in Miami that the director and self-proclaimed 'counterfeit critic' Charles Marowitz persuaded him to discuss the present state of both the active theatre in the West – and of the condition of the critical trade he had once pursued.

IN THE EARLY 'FIFTIES, *when I was stationed in France doing my bit for Uncle Sam, the only thing that kept me sane was my subscription to the* New Republic *and the reviews of Eric Bentley which they contained. In those frosty 'fifties, when the watchword was conformity and the Broadway stage was tamer than the Court Circular in* The Times, *the ring in Bentley's voice made me aware that the theatre could be something more than a combination of warmed-over William Inge and mildly-spiced Robert Anderson – that, as Coriolanus pointed out, 'there is a world elsewhere' and that it contained Expressionism, Russian classics, an English 'new wave', French acting ensembles, and Bertolt Brecht. That was a salvationary insight between 1952 and 1956, and it did a great deal to dignify and aggrandize a theatre that, in the opinion of many of us, was tame, tepid, dreary, and domesticized.*

Since I recently found myself in Miami at the same time as Eric Bentley (he with Lord Alfred's Lover, *I with* Measure for Measure), *I took advantage of the opportunity to pick his brains on a number of subjects of mutual concern. Like all edited transcripts, this is a distillation of a long and woolly conversation.*

Bentley had earlier written in a note to me that writing for the theatre made some kind of sense, but writing about *it no longer did. I began by asking him whether he still held that view.*

It was an impulsive remark inspired to some extent by the hopelessness of the present situation, plus the fact that most of the writing about the theatre isn't very good and might as well be forgotten – and in fact, is forgotten about two days after it's been written.

People are always asking: what is the function of theatre criticism? Well, besides providing consumer tips and that sort of thing, I think ideally it should be a discourse, an ongoing discussion of theatrical things, not confined to any one particular review – more a give and take from the entire cultural milieu in which the play is taking place.

Often, it's particularly important in the case of a new author. If you're Ibsen, for instance, coming forward in 1890, someone's bound to say: that's terrible – that's filth, we must stop it. But someone else is going to rise up and mount a heroic defence, and that will be important.

What is the main difference between criticism today and what it was like in the 'fifties when you were reviewing for the New Republic?

I think it's very much the same – certainly in the United States. There are fewer newspapers in New York, of course, but I don't think that makes a very great difference. I saw Brustein argue somewhere that that was a tremendous change, but it wasn't at all – not in the final result. He was arguing, I think, that the *New York Times* now has all the power but, you know, the *New York Times* always had all the power – in fact more, in the days of Brooks Atkinson, because he was looked up to so much more than anybody else.

You don't think it was a corrective, or neutralizing element, that there were six or seven newspapers at that time?

No, because their critics were no good and nobody paid any attention to them.

So even in the 'fifties the Times *was the determining factor?*

Yes, and sometimes if the kind of critic the *Times* liked popped up on another paper, as Walter Kerr did on the *Herald Tribune*, they would simply acquire him.

Tynan talked somewhere about the critic – meaning himself I believe – recording the event for posterity: giving the reader of a future generation some idea of what it was like to be in that particular theatre on that particular night. What do you think ought to be the working premise of the drama critic?

I think that a question like that can only be answered by asking which particular publication a critic is writing for and therefore which public one is addressing.

Why should that make such a difference?

Because you're not performing for *any* audience – you're performing for *this* audience. For instance, if I was writing for the *New Republic*, as I once did, on subjects like Arthur Miller or Lillian Hellman, I would enjoy teasing my readers, who tended to adore or idolize those writers, by being a little mean about them, and thus creating a discourse between us which often resulted in a lot of indignant letters. I knew who I was talking to – I knew what they would consider 'mean'.

The Critic, the Journal, and the Reader

That would seem to suggest that there is such a thing as a definable character to the readership of something like the New York Times *or the* New York Post. *But can such a diffuse metropolitan readership actually be defined ?*

Yes, I hope so. For example, if you're writing for *The Nation*, you're not writing for a New York public, but for a national readership – therefore you're not necessarily writing for people who are going to see the play. That's very different from writing for, let's say, the *Daily News*, where someone is going to pick up that paper in the morning to see if their critic liked the play that opened last night.

The other thing is that although journalists always deny that they are writing down to their public, I think they do. Because they tend to believe that they are superior to their readership, and so there's often a certain dictatorial relationship there. Good criticism can only happen when you're writing for people whom you regard as your peers. You mustn't write down to anyone – or, as for instance Shaw used to do, pretend that his readers were just as witty and refined as himself. God knows they were not!

So sometimes, the critic has to delude himself that he is writing to a more sophisticated public than is actually out there?

If it *is* a delusion. When I was writing for the *New Republic*, my assumption was that my readers were just as sophisticated as I was, although I knew more about theatre specifically because most of them were not theatre people, so I could give information without in any way patronizing them.

Of course your companions on that publication actually set the tone for your reviews: they were themselves astute and sophisticated writers. But, by the same token, a writer for, say, the New York Post *is often surrounded by shlock journalists dealing with popular subjects in a tabloid manner. Do you think that conditions the way a critic's mind works in regard to his readership?*

Pretty much. Once I had a friend, Louis Kronenberger, who was the *Time* magazine critic for several decades. At that time, there was a *Time*-style, more or less dictated by Henry Luce – I think it's largely gone now. Louis resisted that – tried not to write *Time*-style, and told me that he *didn't* write *Time*-style, but in the end, he *did*, and you can see it if, for instance, you compare his reviews with his books, where he was writing freely. You know Shakespeare says the dyer's hand takes on the colour of the dye – that's not a direct quote, just the gist of it. That's very true: that if you work within the framework of a given institution you do become part of it – however independent you may strive to be.

Back to the Realistic Mould?

In the 'sixties there was a strong desire to transcend realism – to get away from the influence of writers such as Miller, Odets, Inge and Williams. There was also a lot of experimentation in non-naturalistic writing – the theatre of the absurd, a lot of talk about 'the death of the word', and so forth. Today, the leading American playwrights are people such as Mamet, Wilson, Shepard, Guare, Baitz, Korder, Henley, Wasserstein. Does that mean that we are back in an unbudgeable realistic mould and can never escape?

Everybody is always rebelling against realism, but it always seems to reassert itself.

And what could be more naturalistic than *Glengarry Glen Ross*, with every third word being 'fuck'? And yet Mamet himself has consciously tried to depart from realism.

There is a kind of belief, isn't there, that by taking naturalistic speech and sculpting it in a kind of Pinteresque way you are somehow transcending realism. Can that really be done?

If you have enough skill. I think certain Irish playwrights, O'Casey in particular, started with Dublin speech and then began playing around with it. He played around with it so much that it became somewhat oratorical and fell into a kind of phoney Irish. It's a difficult proposition because I think the realistic and 'the other' merge or leastways interact a lot.

Does it mean that no matter what we do, we can never really transcend the patterns of psychological realism because they are so much the patterns of the life we know and lead and which the theatre is obliged to reflect – that to try to escape such realism is just so much wasted effort?

I think the the weight of the realistic novel is felt by all of us – Balzac, Tolstoy, these giants who portrayed the world as it is. Playwrights imitated that, and did so rather well – in Ibsen's realistic plays for instance, although he fought against it at the end. Then Brecht arrives, and he doesn't think the theatre is realistic enough. He's going to be *super*-realistic, and other people tend to say those are his departures from realism, that his epic style, his tendency towards 'alienation' are moves away from realism. But since he lived within the aegus of Communism, where social realism was a holy concept, he was obliged to argue: no, no, this is the *real* realism. So ultimately you get lost in a maze of semantics.

Obviously, he had political pressures that he felt he had to accommodate, but he was the only thinker who actually mounted a theory counter to Stanislavsky's.

Against *pyschological* realism but in favour of sociological realism.

Does the fact that it was sociological realism and opposed to facile naturalistic devices make for a fundamental difference?

He thought it was fundamental, but I'm not sure he was right. He liked to say that he didn't merely offer opinions, he offered *truth* – and I think that is what the realists always believed.

The Brechtian Legacy

In the 'sixties and 'seventies Brecht's influence was virtually inescapable, especially in Europe. But now with the dismantling of the Soviet Union and the consequent general disenchantment with both Communism and Marxism, do you think that influence is necessarily going to have to wane?

I think it probably is waning, but I think it could very easily come back. Some of it has to do with just the natural ups and downs of an author's reputation.

But Brecht predicated much of his work on Marxist ideology, and now that Marxism and Communism, its great outgrowth, is falling by the wayside, doesn't it necessarily mean that Brecht has got to fall by the wayside as well?

Only if his practice was consistent with that theory. This is certainly the way he thought and he wanted other people to think in his later decades: but I always assumed he was wrong, and this assumption now works in his favour. The imaginative artist in him was there long before all these theories and was not always consistent with them.

So accidentally he may escape oblivion?

By talent – not by ideology. His notion that it's all part of Marxism and that his work will only succeed as the Soviet Union succeeds is so much political oratory. It never really had any truth, and the Soviet Union never really embraced his work. We can now say that definitively, since there is no longer a Soviet Union.

When his plays were so popular, in the 'sixties and 'seventies, it was a period of great political ferment and Brecht seemed both fashionable and inevitable. But now that we, both in Europe and America, are living in an age of rampaging conservatism, does that not also tend to pull the carpet out from under his plays?

Although I agree with the thrust of what you're saying, I think it's the Other Brecht, not Brecht the social propogandist, who will survive – the Brecht who was there before the Marxist ever arrived. And by that I don't mean to say that nothing will survive but his early works, but that this Other Brecht continued to exist even when he was also spouting Soviet propaganda. It may be that his reputation will now flower more as a lyric poet, since there is a very solid body of poetry there.

I think the plays that simply preach Soviet Communism are his weaker plays. *St. Joan of the Stockyards*, for instance, is philosophically speaking a pathetically inadequate play because it is really saying that if only the Salvation Army would become atheist and join the Communist Party, everything would be fine. But one of the biggest ideological failures of the Soviet Union was atheism – it was regarded as very liberating at one time, but atheism never came to anything. It was as negative as the word sounds. And yet that is a big play which Yale Rep now intends to revive. They would never have done it when the Soviet Union existed because they'd have been too scared, but now they will do it, and I guarantee it will be a dead duck.

Do you think Good Woman of Setzuan, Chalk Circle, *and* Mother Courage *still retain their fundamental validity no matter what changes may take place in the political climate?*

They may have been plotted only as a critique of capitalism but that's not all they are. I think they're a critique of a certain mode of thinking and living and, as such, are still relevant. And by the way, the fact that the Soviet Union is over and that Marxism-Leninism is *perhaps* over – I'm prepared to believe it *is* over – doesn't mean that all the writers will now be saying capitalism is a good thing, the way Mr. Bush and others of his ilk might wish. I think they won't. Capitalism has not shown itself a success because socialism has shown itself a failure. Therefore, a critique of capitalism is still valid.

Postmodernists and Auteurs

How do you explain the phenomenon of performance art – the rise of these many monologists and visually-oriented solo performers? Is this a hangover from the 'sixties Happeners or, even earlier, the Dadaists of the 'twenties, or is it a genuinely new development in theatre?

I see it somewhat negatively. For example, producers love it because they don't have to hire actors – not more than one, anyway. That's a practical point. Not too far from it, there is this tendency among contemporary playwrights to have their plays, all too often, dwindle into monologue. I see it largely as a weakness, although it may have some positive aspects. Of course, there have always been soloists – whether Ruth Draper or Maurice Chevalier or great solo comedians, or even before them the traditional vaudeville monologists. And then, you mustn't forget, there were people like Judy Garland who virtually did her autobiography on stage, pouring out her heartbreak to her fans. No one thought of that as being particularly avant-garde.

If you take into account performers such as Will Rogers, Lenny Bruce, or, as you say, Garland at the Palladium, is it that performance art is only a slight variation on a very old art form, and therefore perhaps a somewhat pretentious label?

That's what I feel about most of this stuff that's considered to be a product of the second part of the twentieth century – including all that's called postmodernism. Postmodernism is an evasive word, you know, because it doesn't tell you what it *is*, only what it's *post*. And it isn't one style, as far as I can make out, or one attitude.

But it's supposed to be eclectic, isn't it?

Then it has to be always eclectic, doesn't it, to be consistent.

The changes which have taken place in the theatre in the past fifty or so years have also affected the classics. Almost every Shakespearean revival nowadays is some kind of auteur-production – conceptualized down to its boots. But is classical work today reflecting the changes that are taking place around us?

It reflects the fact that the serious theatre has become what I call 'universitarian' or overeducated, so that the people in charge feel obliged to contribute their education to whatever they are doing – which wasn't the case in the past when many of them didn't have an education. As late as the Lunts, American actors had no kind of collegiate or university background. Productions didn't have to have what they now call 'concepts': the actors just had to go on and do it.

For instance, in the 'twenties, when I first saw Gielgud's *Hamlet*, people called it 'a very Freudian *Hamlet*'. It was and it wasn't. In the sense that he knew about Freud, well, he didn't – not at that time, he may know something about him now. It was only Freudian if the whole world we lived in was Freudian, if that was the air we breathed. But Gielgud didn't have 'ideas', nor did he expect his director to have any. That was how the theatre was then.

But later on, when you began to get phenomena like the Yale Drama School and the 'profession of the director', which was a relatively new development, and the director had to offer something, which again was new, things began to change. When Salvini did Othello, for instance, he just walked on and did it. There was no theory about blacks or chastity or anything else.

You don't think you could infer a conception that the artist himself had not formulated?

7

Yes, but I think it would have been a traditional one, handed down intuitively, without going through a conscious, cerebral process. Oh yes, if we survey performances of *Hamlet* from the past, someone like Garrick would now be said to have had an interpretation – even though *he* never thought that he did or consciously formulated one. I guess I'm expressing a prejudice. In this area, I favour the intuitive and the traditional over the collegiate or book-nurtured.

But to go back to my last point: can you really make that kind of distinction? I mean Olivier was a rather non-intellectual actor and yet . . . .

Yes, but occasionally he would read a book, or Tynan would provide him with a theory of some sort.

Desecrating the Classics?

But even before Tynan came on the scene, he was doing some pretty interesting conceptual productions of Shakespeare, which I think you're right, he had never mapped out intellectually. But it was there in the work – the instinctive notions produced a conception in the work. I just wonder whether it is ever possible to avoid a 'conception' of a play or a character, even though the act of conception has not consciously been undertaken.

A Victorian actor doing a Shakespearean role was dealing with a great number of inherited ideas. Of course, if they were *all* inherited there would be nothing fresh and people wouldn't say he was marvellous. But why did they think Irving, for example, *was* marvellous? Not because he was the same, but because he was different. Why was he different? Because his vocal characterization was different, he had a different physique, the way he expressed his emotions was different – but not his ideology, because he didn't have one.

Wouldn't his attitude to the role and the time in which he was living have influenced his performance?

But that came about organically – not by conscious design.

Then would you agree that it is unavoidable that every actor is, organically, going to produce a conception of his own?

You can call it that in hindsight but it *wasn't*. It was just a feeling the actor had about what he was doing. I think we ought to let the Shakespeare production develop slowly and organically from within and not, for instance, have a director say: 'I've read Dover Wilson's *What Happens in Hamlet*, and by God, that's the way we're going to do it.' Or worse still, to have someone who is simply in love with his own ingenuity – or worse still again (and this is a prominent trend in modern directing), somebody who wishes to bring a classic down to the people, which usually means bringing it down into the mud, desecrating it, following the modernistic nihilistic tendency to make it filthy or nauseating. That may be putting it too strongly, but when you take an aristocratic form like Mozartian opera, for instance, and set it at a lunch-counter – that is desecration as I see it.

But it's unavoidable, isn't it, that every generation is going to express what's going on in its head through the classics? You bring to my mind the production of Midsummer Night's Dream *which recently played in London where the characters were, in fact, knee-deep in mud a good deal of the time. That caused quite a stir in that it was a visual expression of the play that had not been seen before – at least, not to such an extreme degree. Doesn't something like that justify itself in that the director is clearly refusing merely to repeat the play in a predictable and conventional manner?*

But in the second half of the twentieth century, we haven't had the conventional repetition of the classic. We've had a constant straining for an originality that isn't really there.

Right, point taken. Now can I ask you a much more general question: must there always be a theatre? Can you conceive of a situation in which the theatre might simply disappear – be superceded by the electronic media?

I think the theatre will persist because all through my lifetime people have been saying that the movies or television would remove it and it hasn't happened – not even approximately. In many areas there is more live theatre now, both in the US and in Britain, than when I was growing up.

The Necessary Theatre

Is there something that the theatre can do which is so unique that it can't be done in films or television?

The contact between the live actor and the live spectator.

You don't think that when the electronic media produce first-rate art, as they occasionally do, a contact of that sort is established?

No. Because the spectator can't answer back. He's just glued to the screen.

The theatre spectator doesn't very often answer back either. I mean, in films and television, on an imaginative level, there is the same kind of collaboration, isn't there?

It's a question of interaction. If you substitute a tape for the accompaniment of a song, there's no interaction between you and the orchestra. But when the orchestra is actually out there, reacting to the vicissitudes of each performance, there's a live current out there. Once you've put it on tape, you've killed it.

Could it not be that once you put it on tape you've refined it to its nth degree?

Perhaps, but that would be an alternative, not a replacement. Like Glenn Gould's way of recording piano music – assiduously splicing one version together with another. You know, he's given us compact discs of performances that never really happened but that were carefully scissored together, and there are musicians with more refined tastes than my own who think the results are fantastic. Let's not forbid that. Let's not say an artist mustn't do it. But I don't think that will ever replace a pianist giving a live rendition before a live public.

But if an artist produces the finest definition of his art by working in such a manner, electronically, doesn't that suggest that he can possibly transcend the live experience? Why couldn't what happens in a play be reproduced in a screenplay so well that – I haven't seen Glengarry Glen Ross, for instance , but everyone tells me that the essence of the play is captured on film.

That may be the best way of realizing *that* play. I don't think it would be best for every play. And I think, similarly, an actor like Al Pacino is, from what I know of him, much more effective on screen than he is on stage, so perhaps he should stick to the screen. But there are other actors, of whom Gielgud is perhaps the prime example, who are much weaker on the screen than they are on stage. In a theatre, he has a way of relating to audiences which is clearly not possible in a cinema.

Certainly there are endentured stage actors, and we respond to their work on stage in a way that we do not in any other medium, but I guess what I was really thinking of was the work that is done in the theatre by playwrights, by actors, by directors – the work itself, the artistic composite. What is to prevent that from being so perfectly well translated into another medium that it makes its performance on a stage unnecessary?

I think that may be true for many plays – including some that I've written. There are certain of my plays where all I really need are the actors' heads – not their bodies at all, not their torsos or their legs, let alone their genital organs. Nevertheless I'm not sure that the old plays which were expressly written for the stage are better on the new media. I don't like Shakespeare so well on TV – because they whisper it. Which may be appropriate for television, but that kind of language wasn't written to be whispered.

Don't Olivier's Hamlet *or* Richard III *or even Kenneth Branagh's* Henry V *convey the essence of Shakespeare's plays in an equivalent way – providing at least as much as you usually get in a stage production, and in terms of strong casting a good deal more?*

They may be valid as an alternative, but not as a replacement. I think there's something unique about being in the theatre as the performance is actually unfolding. In the electronic media, there's a layer missing –

What is that?

The electricity passing between the spectator and the actor.

But there is still some degree of electricty, isn't there?

There's no uncertainty. You know that the rest of the film or the tape is there in the can. But on stage, there's always this sense of anticipation – of what will happen next. A 'sense of immediacy' is also part of it – the fact that it's happening now and that the result is uncertain, that there is a palpable transaction taking place right there, at tonight's performance. All of that is psychologically quite important, and seeing a film of it doesn't quite produce the same effect. For instance, it's the actual vibrations between you and me right now which, if we were being filmed, would vanish.

All right, let's take us as a case in point. I'm asking you questions. We're sitting in a room: two real people in a three-dimensional situation. But when this is finished, I will sit down and I will refine and edit this tape in order to make it as coherent as possible. Are you suggesting that the final, coherent, compressed version is going to be less good than the actual experience we are having at the moment?

No, it should be better – but we're not so much interested in the performance aspect of what we're doing as we are in getting a good organization of verbal material.

So our 'theatrical performance' is going to be subordinated to the edited final result. Well, obviously I can't sway you on this point. The theatre is going to live on then, is it?

I'm afraid so.

Leigh Woods

Two-a-Day Redemptions and Truncated Camilles: the Vaudeville Repertoire of Sarah Bernhardt

American vaudeville welcomed a host of important stage actors into its midst during the generation between the mid-1890s and the end of the First World War, and in 1912, following appearances in British music halls, Sarah Bernhardt became vaudeville's centrepiece in its own war with the legitimate theatre for audience and status. By way of exchange, she received the highest salary ever paid to a 'headlined' vaudeville act, while performing a repertoire from which she was able to exclude the sort of light entertainment which had previously typified the medium. Both vaudeville and Bernhardt profited, in very different ways, from this wedding of high culture to low – and in the process a cultural standing seems to have attached itself to exhibitions of pain which legitimised the lot of the morally deviant women she both portrayed and exemplified. Leigh Woods, Head of Theatre Studies at the University of Michigan, explores the ways in which the great actress thus maintained a demand for her services well after the eclipse of her legendary beauty and matchless movement.

SARAH BERNHARDT'S FORAYS into American vaudeville came in lengthy tours while the form was at its height, in 1912-13 and 1917-18, essentially at the same time as the heyday of the British music hall – in which Bernhardt also toured half a dozen times between 1910 and 1920. For her, these tours involved escapes, of a sort, from a legitimate theatre that could no longer easily accommodate her advancing age and worsening health.

Bernhardt's repertoire in vaudeville, although borrowed in part from her legitimate career, is striking for its departure from the generally light tone which the producers and audiences of vaudeville typically favoured. In aggregate, her vaudeville productions offered a grim view of female experience in reiterated and, as time went on, increasingly ritual-like images of masochism and self-destruction.

In what follows, I shall first examine several contexts around Bernhardt's appearances in vaudeville. I shall try to suggest the nature of her appeal in vaudeville, and the appeal of the actress's unconventional repertoire, by vaudeville's standards, to an audience used to making merry. What I hope to unfold here are some of the exactions made on famous actresses in the nineteenth century which were carried over and in some ways intensified in vaudeville until the final years of the First World War.

To some degree, Bernhardt can be seen to have colluded in the processes by which her fame and her notoriety were penalized. She seems to have done so because she knew it was good business, because her options were narrowing, and because marketing bits of her stageworn suffering struck her as the logical and perhaps inevitable extension of her previous career.

The Bill and Its Format

Vaudeville was willing to compromise its roots in popular culture to accommodate the glittering if generally rather coy luminaries it drew away from the legitimate stage. It paid large amounts of money to stage stars, often in excess of what they could have made in 'legit' – and more, too, than all but a handful of the most versatile entertainers trained up in vaudeville could expect to earn. In its taste for stage stars, vaudeville traded something of its reputation as an egalitarian form for the more distinguished profile it displayed while gripping noted actors in its embrace. It also sacrificed something of its trademark in brisk pacing to a group of actors accustomed to more leisurely appearances in generally more gracious and 'respectable' circumstances.

Vaudeville bills after the turn of the century generally comprised between seven and nine elements. Opening acts were called 'doormats' and closing acts 'chasers'. These often consisted of dumb or non-speaking performers whose main function was the utilitarian one of easing audiences into and out of the theatre as part of the quick turn-around dictated by multiple shows daily. The performers in doormats and chasers knew that, because of their placement, they could never expect the audience's full attention, or for that matter any attention at all when the hour was late or the preceding entertainments laggard.

Black performers were often stationed next-to-last, though rarely as 'headliners', because many chasers consisted of animal acts and only the animals could be guaranteed not to complain about following African-Americans on the bill. There was a class system in vaudeville, and stage stars stood at the very top of it, at a great remove from performers who inhabited the levels below them. The stars' very appearances in vaudeville elevated the bills they headed well above the range of standard fare.

These stars found themselves sharing bills with a motley assortment of performers. There were street acts that had developed some kind of specialty; ethnic acts featuring dialect humour to capture Jewish, German, Irish, and Italian immigrants; other ethnic acts in blackface, sometimes African-Americans but more often whites; acrobats, jugglers, aerialists, skaters, and animal-trainers with feats of skill or daring; and supporting players and chorus members appearing in larger and showier vaudeville productions, but lacking stars of magnitude. Song-and-dance acts were common, often including a performer of each sex. After 1910

or so, non-dialect comedians became vaudeville staples, too, often in double acts of laugh-getter and straight man (or woman).

All headliners from the stage found themselves either in the spot just before intermission or next-to-last on their vaudeville bills. The next-to-last act fell after the audience returned from the intermission, and had usually seen another filler act to settle them back into their seats. After the traditional headliner's slot, then, the audience was primed to leave the theatre either during the chaser or just after it.

The Role of the Star

Stage stars like Bernhardt with heavy sets always played in the next-to-last slot because the time needed to arrange the stage could only come during the intermission. The slot following just after intermission was a particularly tough one, sandwiched as it was between the two most prestigious acts on the bill. This act fulfilled a function in some ways like the opening and closing acts before an audience that was restless, distracted, and looking forward to the headliner.

All acts were short. Doormats and chasers often ran ten minutes or less. Longer acts lasted between twenty and thirty minutes, and fell in the featured slots – usually four, five, and seven. Occasionally, a stage star's play would last longer than half an hour, but given vaudeville's brisk and insistent rhythms, such a length could carry risks. In fact, the most common criticisms of stage stars in vaudeville damned them for action that took too long in getting under way.

Vaudeville audiences also expected that a star would be on stage when the play began, or enter very soon afterwards. This expectation either accelerated or erased entirely a practice prevalent in the legitimate theatre of the day, that had the star's character discussed at length by the other characters before that star made her triumphal appearance.

Slots in the less prominent parts of the vaudeville bill were often juggled by local managers after the first weekly matinee on Monday. When changes were made in a stage star's bill, this often took the form of shuffling the acts on either side of the star, so as to manipulate the audience into the proper frame of mind just before or after the headlined act appeared. A performer doing a dumb act to open for Bernhardt might well have been a headliner many times at a smaller theatre, sometimes only the week before.

Nevertheless, the class and salary system in vaudeville related very directly to slots on the bill, and to the prestige of the theatre where the bill was playing. There was truth in Channing Pollock's jest, written in 1911, that when it came to vaudevillians, 'By their numbers ye shall know them.'[1] Performers grew accustomed to thinking of themselves as numbers in their slot on the bill, in the minutes that their acts took up, and in their weekly salaries. Vaudeville showed a passion for quantification that affected all levels of the enterprise.

A kind of mechanized quality that seemed brisk and efficient to vaudeville audiences did not always seem so to stars accustomed to the legitimate theatre. Mrs. Patrick Campbell, famed from legit in A. W. Pinero's *The Second Mrs. Tanqueray*, complained of the trials she suffered during her single short tour of vaudeville in 1910: 'Oh, those two [daily] performances. . . . I had to kill a man twice a day and shriek – and it had to be done from the heart – the Americans see through "bluff" – and I was advertised as a "Great tragic actress"!'[2] Ethel Barrymore found touring difficult at a time when she had young children. But she remembered her tours later for the way that, in vaudeville, 'Things ran as systematically and efficiently as in a large business concern', training up an 'audience . . . so used to perfection that they are tough.'[3]

Jessie Millward, a British actress who specialized in melodrama, grew frazzled by the travel and the mechanized vaudeville routine. In her case, though, her first tours were short ones – only the several blocks between F. F. Proctor's Fifth Avenue and his Twenty-Third Street theatres in New York City in 1904. Then again, Millward played two shows in each theatre for a total of four

shows daily, racing from one theatre to another for both matinee and evening performances in order to fill spots on the two different bills:

When the first week of it was over, I caught myself jumping out of bed in the middle of nights and rushing to the door mechanically as if I were going to take another car to somewhere or other. It was an experience that I certainly shall never go through again. Hereafter, I shall be content to appear in one theatre at a time, giving two performances, of course, each day, but not in places several miles apart [*sic*].[4]

Millward's nightmare resembles what performers in small time vaudeville experienced routinely, doing as many as five or six shows per day. On the other hand, Millward became the first actress to make $1000 a week in vaudeville in a development which in some ways presaged Bernhardt's interest and eventual appearance in the form. But Millward's salary and her mode of travel would both find themselves outstripped eight years later, when Bernhardt entered the field.

Bernhardt Enters Vaudeville

Extensive travel was built into vaudeville, with large circuits of its theatres coming under the control of a handful of monopolistic producers during the dozen years that followed the turn of the century. Extensive travel suited Bernhardt, part of whose celebrity derived from popular images of her itinerancy and rootlessness as an artist, and from the grand manner in which she travelled with her entourages. She made several world tours during her legitimate career, and the one that began in 1891 lasted over two years, taking her across the United States and Canada, to Hawaii, Samoa, New Zealand, and Australia, then back to the United States, off to France and London, to Belgium, the Netherlands, Luxembourg, Switzerland, Czechoslovakia, Poland, Russia, Austria, Italy, Monaco, the French Riviera, on to a jaunt that included Hungary, Romania, Turkey, Greece, and Portugal, and then to a final leg with stops in Brazil, Argentina, and Senegal.[5]

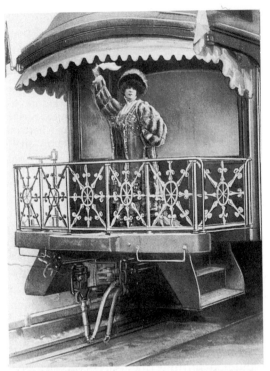

Top: a buoyant Bernhardt at the back of her train (Sanders Collection, University of Michigan).
Bottom: Lillie Langtry with Bernhardt (Players Club).

Lacking the model domestic life that drove and at the same time confined the American star Ethel Barrymore's stints in vaudeville to locations mostly in and around New York City, Bernhardt may even have welcomed the prospect of entering its farthest reaches at such a late stage in her career. She certainly welcomed the $7000 a week she earned during her first tour and (with a war on) the $5500 a week she made during her second vaudeville engagement.

Because vaudeville offered cheap daily matinees and relatively low prices for its evening shows, women were often more heavily represented in its audiences than they were in legitimate theatres of the time. This element of vaudeville seems to have suited it to female performers in general and ageing actresses in particular. The spectacle of the late-sixtyish and then finally seventy-ish Bernhardt on two long marches through vaudeville recalled that offered by the not-quite-so-matronly Lillie Langtry. Langtry was also internationally famous from a long touring career and the days of her earlier attachment – shared later by her friend Bernhardt – to the Prince of Wales, Queen Victoria's son Albert Edward, who later became Edward VII of England.

In the legitimate theatre, Langtry had specialized in worldy-wise, bejewelled characters in comic or satiric pieces. Her vaudeville offerings, however, located themselves much more firmly in a retrograde morality. *Between Nightfall and the Light* and *The Test* were both excerpted from her legitimate success in the 1880s in Victorien Sardou's *A Wife's Peril*, and during her first and second vaudeville tours respectively each play had Langtry's character dying at the hands of her would-be-seducer after having been tempted to infidelity by him with the news of her own husband's philandering. On her third and final vaudeville tour, Langtry alternated in *Ashes* and *The Eleventh Hour*, in both of which she featured as an erring and anxious wife. Here, her characters did not die, but were chastened rather – and determined to expiate their lapses from domestic propriety.

Bernhardt's vaudeville repertoire showed even greater licence – and greater severity.

She had first played Marguerite Gautier, the Camille in *La Dame aux Camélias* by Alexandre Dumas *fils*, in the United States during her first tour there in 1880.[6] When originally in America, Bernhardt had been amused to learn that schoolchildren were forbidden to see her as Camille; in France, though she had still not played the role there, she knew that children attended matinees of Dumas' play as a rite of passage in their educations.[7] In any case, her characterization of Camille made a sensation in the United States, only later becoming one in Europe. Over time, it came to stand as the prototype of an undomesticated and therefore rootless woman falling victim to the tortures of love.

Vaudeville thus afforded Bernhardt and Langtry outlets for their notoriety in ways the legitimate stage did not. And in its hypocritical and self-serving attempts to serve up 'family' entertainment, vaudeville offered an arena where a sort of confused and titillating Victorianism prevailed. Such values permitted sexual reference and erotic innuendo – never more so than when these could be instantly juxtaposed, in plays lasting only about half an hour, with suffering and very often death.

Bernhardt's First Repertoire

More than thirty years after she first played the role, Bernhardt made Camille, the only part she played on both her tours, her most durable attraction in vaudeville. Furthermore, during her first tour no fewer than four of the other five pieces she played portrayed women victimized by the strength or expression of their love. The fifth role was from her own son's play, *Une Nuit de Noël sous la terreur*, in which romantic love did not figure prominently. On the other hand, Maurice, as Bernhardt's illegitimate son, was the living emblem of the actress's much-publicized erotic history.

Besides *Camille* and Maurice's, her other plays included Jean Racine's seventeenth-century classic *Phèdre*, Victor Hugo's *Lucrèce Borgia*, and Sardou's *La Tosca* and *Théodora*. Bernhardt had played all of these at full

Top: Bernhardt in *Une Nuit de Noël sous la terreur*.
Bottom: Bernhardt as Camille. (Sanders Collection.)

length in the legitimate theatre: indeed, the roles in Sardou's plays had been written for her in the first place. In choosing portions of the full-length pieces for her brief appearances in vaudeville, Bernhardt fixed on the climactic episodes of plays which – like *Camille* but excluding *Phèdre*, where she played the first two acts only – included her characters' deaths. Even her extract from *Phèdre*, though, included her spurned character's invitation to her beloved stepson to kill her with his sword.

Such plays and such outcomes stood squarely in line with notions of gender in the late nineteenth century. Here, Bronson Howard describes a scenario common on legitimate stages during the last two decades of the century, and his sense of poetic justice would extend itself in vaudeville in the hands of Bernhardt and some of the other female stage stars who entered it. According to Howard, himself a playwright of note:

In England and America, the death of a pure woman on the stage is not 'satisfactory', except when the play rises to the dignity of tragedy. The death, in an ordinary play, of a woman who is not pure, as in the case of *Frou-Frou* [by Meilhac and Halévy, in which Bernhardt had also created the title role], is perfectly satisfactory, for the reason that it is inevitable. . . . The wife who has once taken the step from purity to impurity can never reinstate herself in the world of art on this side of the grave; and so an audience looks with complacent tears on the death of an erring woman.[8]

Bernhardt chose a sequence of roles for herself in vaudeville modelled on a formula rooted thirty years earlier, when she had first played Camille, having also taken many similar roles in her earlier and later legitimate career. In vaudeville, however, the permutations these parts found in bills through the course of several weeks, and the compression in suffering they assumed by being cut to conform to vaudeville's exacting time limit, rendered their cautionary qualities the more conspicuous.

Bernhardt was unique among the serious actors who entered vaudeville in alternating several different pieces there. Other stars lacked her repertoire of short pieces and her skill in playing them, perfected over the previous thirty years of her career from the continental practice of touring in several pieces rather than in one. Other actresses of note also lacked her skill in putting over (and varying) outcomes involving loving too much or 'wrongly', and the consequent suffering and death.

Alternating in a number of pieces gave Bernhardt and the vaudeville producers a strategy for drawing more spectators to see her – one night as Camille, the next as Phèdre, and so on; but this cycle was transformed through the course of vaudeville's fourteen weekly shows into a litany of womanly love's most dire consequences.

The Repertoire for the Second Tour

This same pattern fell out during her subsequent tours in vaudeville, even when her repertoire changed. In 1917-18 Bernhardt often doubled Camille with Alexandre Bisson's *Madame X* within single weeks and, sometimes, even on single bills during the legitimate engagements she sometimes interspersed with her appearances in vaudeville. *Madame X* treated a wife who had deserted her husband and young son only to be reunited years later with that son, who comes by chance to defend her against a murder charge. Madame X, like Camille, dies morally absolved and quite ecstatic at the end of her play.

In 1915 – the year after the First World War began and two years after her first tour of vaudeville ended – Bernhardt's right leg was amputated. Not only did this confine her to the brief *tours de force* she had been refining as her staple for English music halls since 1910, but it forced her to change an acting style which had been marked for many years by a quality of movement some had called feline, some serpentlike, and which all agreed was heavily charged with erotic associations.

Having to perform under this limitation seems only to have enlarged her taste for the heroic and the sacrificial. On her final tour, with the First World War raging, she paired 'a French Countess who refused to leave her

Bernhardt's vaudeville roles, as illustrated in the souvenir programme. Top left: as Phèdre. Top right: as Lucrèce Borgia. Bottom left: as Tosca. Bottom right: as Theodora. (Sanders Collection, University of Michigan.)

chateau during the German invasion and gave shelter to wounded French and American soldiers', from *Arrière les Huns*,[9] with the role in another patriotic vehicle, *Du Théatre au champs d'honneur*, of a mortally wounded young man on the battlefield, 'a former actor and poet . . . determined to save his battalion's flag from enemy hands.'[10]

At other times, Bernhardt doubled on vaudeville bills as the doomed son of Napoleon in the last act of Edmond Rostand's *L'Aiglon* and as the title character in Maurice Bernhardt's *La Mort de Cléopâtre*. At still others, she paired the dying Cleopatra with the martyr in Emile Moreau's *Le Procès de Jeanne d'Arc*.

Thus, Bernhardt brought into vaudeville for her final tour two male roles plus a third, Joan of Arc, with masculine qualities. She had done this earlier in her career, even playing Hamlet in one controversial engagement that took her to both Paris and London. Far from escaping the prototypical suffering woman's experience in such roles, though, Bernhardt suffered and died – or in the case of her Joan saw herself railroaded toward death – in all of them.

Thus, in a theatrical femininity that had by this time become emblematic, Bernhardt on the one hand applied herself to suffering in a universal way, with warfare as the male equivalent of her female characters' martyrdoms to romance; on the other, her male characters and Bernhardt's Joan of Arc were ennobled by a heroism seen to benefit entire nations. The roles were consequently imbued with a kind of altruism that departed in some ways from what in Bernhardt's time were often called 'soiled doves', so willing to die for the men they loved.

The 'Weekly Laugh Bulletin' of the *New York Star* anatomized Bernhardt's performance as Joan of Arc at the Palace Theatre, New York, for the week ending 6 January 1918, pinning down the actress and her production in its customarily clinical and quantified way. Under 'Reception' it noted that Bernhardt's had been 'Big'; under 'Applause', 'Good'; under 'Laughs', not surprisingly, '0'; under 'Finished', again 'Big'; and under 'Acting Time', '31 minutes'.

Sandwiched between a song-and-dance act and a comedian at the Wednesday matinee, Sarah's initial reception took top honours, but Rooney and Bent before her and Harry Fox following her gathered twenty-one and twenty-two laughs respectively, and Rooney and Bent finished 'excellent', according to the *Star*.[11] Their exit in *Up Town* surpassed and set up the less conventional and more equivocal vaudeville 'finish' that Bernhardt offered her audiences. Vaudeville's passion for quantification seems to have set the actress's suffering as Joan at a comfortable distance – and perhaps was what made it tolerable. Furthermore, her Joan had been only one element on the bill, complemented and in some ways compromised by the laughs that came before and after it.

The Legend Appropriated

In one respect, Bernhardt seems to have mined a vein in her vaudeville pieces which already existed in her legitimate repertoire – and which she did not need to look very hard to find. More surprisingly, though, vaudeville seems to have furnished her with a climate that suited the suffering characters in her repertoire. And so sisters-in-pain to her Camille were taken up by other actresses who toured in vaudeville before and after her.

Valerie Bergere, another French actress, tailored Camille for American consumption in her vaudeville sketch called *A Bowery Camille*. Camille was played on the legitimate stage by Virginia Harned, Nance O'Neil, Clara Morris, Olga Nethersole, Mrs. Leslie Carter, and Ethel Barrymore – to list only those most noted among the actresses like Bernhardt who came to vaudeville from the stage. But none chose to play Camille in vaudeville – the role was too strongly associated with Bernhardt after the late 1880s – though all but Barrymore moved into the form with the savour of this kind of role around her.

Vaudeville marketed Bernhardt's profile and her line of suffering women in other ways, too. Thus, when Olga Nethersole came into vaudeville in 1913-14, the year after Bernhardt's first tour, she was billed as 'the British Bernhardt'. A certain derivative quality showed itself in the way Nethersole took her curtain calls after playing Sapho, another libidinous and subsequently repentant character. *Variety* derided Nethersole for her numerous 'unnatural Bernhardt bows' in vaudeville.[12] Earlier, Mrs. Leslie Carter had been labelled 'the American Bernhardt', after her turn-of-the-century success as the loose-living music hall artiste, Zaza.[13] She later took Zaza, or as it might have been called, 'the American Camille', into vaudeville with her.

David Warfield, subsequently a star in his own right, came up in vaudeville in the late 1880s. He confessed many years afterward that his early appearance at The Wigwam, a vaudeville house in San Francisco, had included, among other things, 'imitations of Bernhardt, Irving, and Salvini. Bernhardt I had never seen, but that did not bother me – I created a burlesque of her in *Camille*.'[14] Warfield's resourcefulness prefigured Bernhardt's appearances in vaudeville, while those of Nethersole and Carter were in some ways predicated on Bernhardt's, suggesting the multifarious ways her most famous role was appropriated by public and peers alike.

Perhaps anticipating the audience's sure interest in her storied appearance, Bernhardt joked about the weight she had put on prior to her first tour in vaudeville. At the age of sixty-eight, she knew she would be playing several women jeopardized by love on the tour besides Camille. Her bantering with interviewers suggests that she took it as her strategy to prime her first vaudeville audiences to be pleasantly surprised at her appearance.[15]

She certainly used the clever costuming and lighting for which she was known to enhance her appeal. She took pains over the look of her shows far in excess of vaudeville's customary expectations, with one critic praising her productions for their ability 'to create illusion and to banish the vaudeville atmosphere'.[16]

As her later vaudeville appearances began to assume the tone of valedictories, creating 'illusion' appears to have become even more crucial. Bernhardt had been playing Camille for nearly forty years by 1917, and observers of some of her later performances noticed her using her leading man's arm to break her final death-fall[17] – a sensible choice for an ailing and finally one-legged actress.

Roles of Emblematic Suffering

The cutting for vaudeville prefaced Camille's death perfunctorily, with only enough music and dialogue to set the moment up. But Bernhardt's Camille lent itself to abbreviation in its familiarity to many audience members and in her long association with the role – including a filmed appearance in Dumas *fils'* play prior to taking Camille into vaudeville.

It was as though Bernhardt was finally able to serve up her Camille in a kind of shorthand, taking for granted her audience's knowledge of the story and her own history in the role. In this way, she used Camille and her long tenure in it as emblems of suffering and, paradoxically, of the transcendence of her acting. Of course, her suffering in Camille and similar roles was precisely what rendered them transcendent in Bernhardt's eyes and, to judge the matter from a steady demand for such roles in vaudeville, in the eyes of her audiences as well.

Furthermore, the magnitude and long-standing nature of Bernhardt's celebrity lent her acting considerable transparency by the time she hit vaudeville. This left her, in many minds as well as her own, indistinguishable from the most recurrent among her roles. She had figured prominently in no fewer than five *romans à clef* over the years, including Alphonse Daudet's *Le Nabab* (1876), Edmond de Goncourt's *La Faustin* (1881), Félicien Champsaur's *Dinah Samuel* (1880s), Jean Lourain's *Le Tréteau* (1906), and most sensationally in *Les Memoirs de Sarah Barnum* (1883) by her fellow-actress and former friend, Marie Colombier.[18]

It is fitting that Colombier should have conflated Bernhardt with America's circus master and huckster-supreme, P. T. Barnum, the analogy anticipating Bernhardt's huge appeal in vaudeville three decades later. By then, American press agentry had been grafted onto 'vaudeville' – the very term borrowed, for the sophistication and respectability it carried with it, from the French, in something of the way vaudeville, in Francophilic fashion, deployed Bernhardt's prestige for its own cultural aggrandisement.

Perhaps the most famous fictional realization of Bernhardt fell in writing of a much higher order than the *romans à clef* – in Marcel Proust's *The Remembrance of Things Past*, through the character of the actress Berma. Bernhardt's loftier cultural associations lent her presence even greater appeal in vaudeville, ever eager as it was to offer something for everyone – and, in Bernhardt's case, to raise its ticket prices in the process. Still the most famous performer in the world, Bernhardt legitimated a new scale when she commanded a top price of $2.50 for her three and a half weeks at the Palace in May 1913, furnishing testimony of the more monied kind of patron she succeeded in drawing into vaudeville in her capacious wake.[19]

Acting Out Mortality

Circumstances perhaps gave Bernhardt more powerful grounds for the conflation of her life with her art as that life drew to its close. A young anaesthetist who assisted at the actress's amputation – which fell between the two vaudeville tours – kept notes of the event:

At 10 A.M. the great artist was wheeled into the operating room. She was dressed in a white satin peignoir and swathed in pink crepe-de-chine veils. She seemed very calm. . . . Turning to [*the surgeon*] Denucé she said: 'My darling, give me a kiss.' Then to me, 'Mademoiselle, I'm in your hands. Promise you'll really put me to sleep. Let's go, quickly, quickly.' In all this one could not help see the tragedienne putting on an act. I felt I was at the theatre except that I myself had a role in the painful drama. . . . The wound is dressed and the great tragedienne, crowned by her peignoir and satin-lined sheepskin, is wheeled back to her room. When she is in bed she screams: 'I want my beloved son, my

Maurice, my darling child!' He kisses her, saying: 'Maman, you look just fine, you're all right, all right.' 'Where is Denucé and the young woman who put me to sleep?' 'Madame, I am here', I said. 'Ah, darling, you're nice. Come here. I want to see you.' I try to leave but she detains me. 'Darling', she says, 'I like you, stay a bit longer.' I tell her to be calm and not to talk. 'I'm talking because I must speak a little. Oh, I'm suffering, suffering.' The drama continues. One feels she is always acting, playing the role of someone who has just undergone a grave operation.[20]

The anaesthetist, like the vaudeville audience, was aware of Bernhardt's standing and eager to preserve it so as to lend value to her own presence at a significant event. The actress's mortality is the background against which both Bernhardt as its possessor and purveyor, and her portable audience as its morbid consumer, judges the significance of the performance. Bernhardt was acting out her own death, after a fashion, as she did in vaudeville both before and after her operation in anticipation of a real death which did not come until 1923. She seems also to have been casting her surgeon, Denucé and even her own son, Maurice, as operating room Armands to her stricken Camille.

Bernhardt had great gifts as a comic actress, but this was clearly not the expressive idiom she developed as she aged, nor the mode that her later audiences preferred. Comedy was, on the other hand, precisely the vocabulary taken up by 'the American Bernhardt', Mrs. Leslie Carter, when her Camille-like Zaza took her through her first vaudeville tour in 1915-16. In her vaudeville version of Zaza, she was criticized for doing 'considerable "comeding" that would put [the low comedienne] Marie Dressler or Charles Chaplin to shame.'[21] Then, in the 'twenties, Mrs. Carter played a series of character roles on the legitimate stage, such as Lady Kitty in Somerset Maugham's *The Circle* in New York, in which she could lampoon her earlier glamour and sensuous allure.

Lillie Langtry also ventured into comedy in vaudeville during her second tour in 1912-13 – seeking, perhaps, to avoid overt comparisons with Bernhardt, whom she

Bernhardt at the close of her final vaudeville tour, in 1918 (Hampden-Booth Theatre Library, Players Club).

knew would be touring at the same time. Langtry took roles as suffragists and independent women, first in *Helping the Cause*, and later, after returning to her staple errant wife in *The Test*, in *Mrs. Justice Drake*, a play according to one critic, 'full of prankish situations arising from the regime of the suffragettes.'[22]

Her success in this piece on the western part of her tour in some ways redeemed Langtry's dismal failure in *Helping the Cause*, which was received 'coldly' at the Brooklyn Orpheum and was later closed down in mid-run by the manager of Pittsburgh's Grand Theatre. For her final tour in 1915-16, Langtry went back to erring wives, although she avoided fatal endings, and then retired after one more engagement at English music halls in 1918.

Olga Nethersole, 'the British Bernhardt', retired at the end of her only vaudeville tour in 1914. Bernhardt might have done the same, but instead she did one more tour in England, including some music halls there after her last stint in vaudeville in America. She was acting in a film in France, at a studio fashioned in her own lodgings within days of her death. Produced by a Hollywood company, *La Voyante*, with Bernhardt as the title character, was about a clairvoyant who told the future from Tarot cards.[23]

The Irony of 'Independence'

Although Bernhardt ended her career playing a character looking into the future, her vaudeville phase referred in more ways to the past. Jean Cocteau wrote that 'by her extraordinary power of swooning she filled the arms of the world'.[24] Unconsciousness or death, with its savour of vulnerability, was the only release for most of the characters she played in vaudeville. Such extreme conditions proved to be Bernhardt's only release from acting, too – the career that gave her much freedom, but only, it would seem, of a certain sort. In this regard, her time in vaudeville and the conclusion to her career stand distinct among her contemporaries and fellow actresses.

Bernhardt's appearances in vaudeville suggest that a popular entertainment, in a way not unrelated to its escapist tendencies and more malleable cultural presence, can reaffirm values at risk of unravelling – even, and perhaps especially in the person of such a negative exemplar as Sarah Bernhardt. Vaudeville did not always fill a recuperative function, particularly when employing the younger, jazzier entertainers it had itself trained up: but it joined in a reactionary stance with the renowned Bernhardt to recommend, through a series of admonitory outcomes for otherwise highly attractive characters, a narrow morality for women and the mortal penalty for deviations from such morality.

With the plays she chose to present in vaudeville, Bernhardt seems to have referred her audiences quite wittingly to her own romantic past, chequered with affairs with actors, men of letters, statesmen, members of the nobility, and occasionally, it was rumoured, other women.[25] Her personal life lent her a certain allure, but it seems also to have engendered an expectation that she would redeem such licence on the stage and pay for it in some way later in her life.

The valedictory appearances Bernhardt made in vaudeville, gauged in the context first of her growing incapacity, and finally of the amputation of her leg, represented a sort of public repentance even while they offered her huge financial rewards. By acting in a larger touring repertoire than any other actor to come into vaudeville, she was able to capitalize on the image of 'variety' that had marked vaudeville from its inception – and, perhaps, on her own sense of acting as 'a feminine art'.[26]

On the other hand, she found herself late in her career speaking a language that few among her audiences could understand – even while invoking moral assumptions around women, in their freedom and capacity to express love, that appear to have been so ingrained and transcultural as to have been taken for granted by all parties concerned. In this connection, her vaudeville repertoire was not as liberating or as liberated as it might have seemed in the 1880s.

It is ironic that this process should have depended on an actress whose career and personal life were viewed by so many of her contemporaries as models of personal initiative and independence. This dramatizes the degree to which Bernhardt found herself captivated – and in her later years driven – by a repertoire that held such appeal to audiences in vaudeville. Indeed, Bernhardt's vaudeville repertoire was even more striking, set into fare that magnified even while it trivialized the actress's virtuosity in suffering and pain.

None of the most famous male stage actors to enter vaudeville played death scenes. Among the women, only Virginia Harned, a minor star, who played the title role in an adaptation of Tolstoy's *Anna Karenina* in vaudeville, and the Russian expatriate Alla Nazimova, who played a character who committed suicide at the end of Marion Craig Wentworth's *War Brides*, could approach the gravity of Bernhardt's scenarios.

In short, only women – and foreign ones at that among the major stars – were qualified to enact death on the vaudeville stage. Their ignorance of the American form's prevailing escapism may have been conceded, or they may have been granted the right to perform their heavy pieces in deference to their international stature. Even more broadly, suffering unto death may have seemed to vaudeville's producers, and to many among its audiences too, the proper expressive preserve of women.

Nazimova was only thirty-six when she appeared in *War Brides*, though, and so the impact of her character's death seems to have signified something quite different than it did in the venerable Bernhardt's battery of doomed characters. In Bernhardt's case, vaudeville audiences seem to have taken voyeuristic fascination in a famous actress's willingness to expose her body as a simulacrum of her state in life, and in a kind of public penance for the life she was known

to have led. The frankness of this exchange defined vaudeville as a more 'popular' form in its day than the legitimate theatre was or than it wanted to be.

Notes and References

1. Channing Pollock, *The Footlights Fore and Aft* (Boston: Richard G. Badger, 1911), p. 339.
2. Mrs. Patrick Campbell [Beatrice Stella Cornwallis-West], *My Life and Some Letters* (London: Hutchinson, 1922), p. 240.
3. Ethel Barrymore, *Memories* (New York: Harper and Brothers, 1955), p. 177-8.
4. The Robinson Locke Collection, 'Jessie Millward', unidentified clipping dated 19 June 1904, Envelope 1478, Billy Rose Theatre Collection of the New York Public Library at Lincoln Center, New York City.
5. Cornelia Otis Skinner, *Madame Sarah* (Boston: Houghton Mifflin, 1966), p. 280-2.
6. Arthur Gold and Robert Fizdale, *The Divine Sarah: a Life of Sarah Bernhardt* (New York: Alfred A. Knopf, 1991), p. 172.
7. Gold and Fizdale, p. 170.
8. Bronson Howard, *The Autobiography of a Play* (New York: Columbia University, 1914); p. 27-8; from Howard's lecture given first in 1886, and repeated in 1889.
9. From an unidentified obituary of Bernhardt at the Firestone Library, Princeton University, Princeton, New Jersey.
10. Skinner, p. 324.
11. 'Bernhardt', undated clipping, Vol. 68, Locke Collection.
12. 'Olga Nethersole', clipping dated 10 October 1913, Vol. 364, Locke Collection.
13. 'Mrs. Leslie Carter', Vol. 27, Locke Collection.
14. David Warfield, 'My Own Story', *McClure's*, XLIX (September 1917), p. 15.
15. 'Bernhardt', Vol. 66, Locke Collection.
16. Ibid.
17. Gerda Taranow, *Sarah Bernhardt: the Art within the Legend* (Princeton: Princeton University Press, 1972), p. 94.
18. Gold and Fizdale, p. 27, 116, 207.
19. Charles and Louise Samuels, *Once upon a Stage: the Merry World of Vaudeville* (New York: Dodd, Mead, 1974), p. 261.
20. Gold and Fizdale, p. 317.
21. 'Mrs. Leslie Carter', clipping from *Variety* dated 19 February 1915, Vol. 27, Locke Collection.
22. 'Langtry', Vol. 310, Locke Collection.
23. Skinner, p. 330.
24. Quoted in Gold and Fizdale, p. 302.
25. Gold and Fizdale, p. 134.
26. Sarah Bernhardt, *The Art of the Theatre*, trans. Henry James Stenning (1924; reprinted, New York: Benjamin Blom, 1969), p. 144.

Arthur H. Ballet

After-Dinner Thoughts of America's Oldest Living Dramaturg

Arthur Ballet was a dramaturg in America before the English-language theatre really knew that such a theatrical functionary had long been leading a curious backstairs life in the theatres of central Europe. He directed and taught theatre at the University of Minneapolis for many years until, in 1961, he became Director there of the grandly-entitled Office for Advanced Drama Research – in which capacity he not only gave unstintingly of time and advice to hundreds of aspirant playwrights, but guided their work towards likely outlets, and selected and edited no fewer than thirteen volumes of new work in the *Playwrights for Tomorrow* series. He was also a regular dramaturg for the O'Neill Playwrights' Conference, and later served in that role at the Guthrie Theatre. During the Carter years Arthur Ballet was director of the theatre programme for the National Endowment for the Arts. In 1975 he became an advisory editor of *Theatre Quarterly*, as he has been of NTQ from our first issue. What follows is an after-dinner speech made to an association whose very existence would have seemed an improbability just a few decades ago – the Literary Managers and Dramaturgs of the Americas, to whom he here addresses some words of practical advice and cautionary wisdom.

I THANK YOU ALL for inviting me to share my thoughts with you. I suspect I may abuse your hospitality and upset some of you, perhaps all of you. If so, I apologise in advance, but I also hope that I do not bore you. At least not too much.

My ramblings this evening must begin with a question: why in the hell are we so serious? Dare I go on? So serious, so pompous, so angry, so pretentious, so portentious? If theatre isn't joyous, fun for us, then how on earth can we expect it to be so for our audiences? Yes, I am aware that our roots are in ritual, in religious gatherings, in perhaps solemn assemblages, but I am willing to lay odds that there was some hanky-panky backstage at the theatres of Dionysus, and that even those Central and South American priests tossing youngsters into pits of fire were doing so with giggles and a sense of: hey now, *that's* theatrical!

At the same time, as I keep saying to anyone who will listen to me, our theatrical ancestors were charlatans, tumblers, snake-oil salesmen, impresarios in fedoras and fur-collared coats, and con men who neverthe-less *delighted in entertaining* and in making a buck (often dishonestly) on the side or up front. Our predecessors in short were fakers, pretenders, who must have enjoyed themselves as they fleeced the crowd.

Nowadays as I wander in theatre offices and backstage, there seems to be very little joy or laughter, and even less willingness to admit that we are enjoying the fakes we are palming off on the audience. I look at the programme notes that you, my colleagues, have prepared so laboriously, so intelligently, so earnestly, and I have to wonder who reads them . . . and why?

Oh, I know that middle Europeans and some theatre people set great store by these notes, but my observations would indicate that bored audiences rifle through programmes reading the cast lists, all the explanations of what the plot is about, and the 'notes' . . . all this after they have inspected the ads. But remember these are the people who have lost interest in the comings and the goings on the stage.

We are so intent on concept, on 'meaning', and on being taken seriously as a profession and as artisans creating art that we forget that the whole art form is one of fakery, and that we are deceivers (some gay and some not). I would add that we seem to fear not being respectable and somehow educational and important. And so we load our programmes with respectable research.

I put forward these notions because I am concerned that our audiences are responding without joy, without excitement, while theatre in some cities is in danger of becoming a classroom and a dull one at that. As a teacher for thirty-five years of an enormous introduction to the theatre class, I quicky learned one important thing from the students: keep 'em laughing and then punch home the critical tidbit: if you will, laughter may lead to the moment of truth, if there is one. Pomposity and earnestness will not.

Moving right along, I am saddened to find that playwrights by and large don't want *us*. At least they seem to reject us once we have recommended their plays to the artistic director. And I wonder why. Maybe the answer is that we have become scolding schoolteachers bent on correcting quizzes. I hate to say this, but I think we have become literary scholars rather than theatrical magicians: our senses and our defences are becoming largely pedantic rather than truly dramatic.

I would suggest that playwrights of course need dramaturgs, as do directors, but they need us as supportive resources, not as antagonists. They need to learn to trust us – and for them to trust us, we had damned well better earn that trust by knowing *theatre*, and the gimmicks and trickery of theatre. Perhaps we should stop worrying so much about meaning, about social and psychological guilts, and worry more about what 'works' theatrically.

I have often puzzled (as I trod on through all this over the years) about the fashionable play-of-the-year. You know, the play that every theatre in the country clamours to 'do' and to do *now*. After a plethora of productions of these trendy pieces, most are quickly forgotten because, quite frankly, there isn't much in them to remember, to return to, to think about, to produce again.

Oh you want names? Sure. *That Championship Season, I'm Not Rappaport, Driving Miss Daisy, Steel Magnolias, The Heidi Chronicles* – for starters. I think they all will fall into the bin of lost plays in a year or so, as some already have.

And then some conscientious literary manager will 'find' one of these 'lost' plays and plug it at a meeting about the upcoming season. I am talking now of the year 2050, let's say. They will forget that plays are lost because, by and large, they deserve to be forgotten. Oh not all of them, but many of them. Anyway in 2050 I won't be around for you to point out my miscalculations.

About critics: stop quoting them and stop fighting with them. We have no more right to tell the newspapers who their critics should be than they have a right to tell us what plays to do or who should direct them. If there are (and heaven knows there *are*) incompetent reviewers, there are also incompetent directors, actors, and even, dare I say, dramaturgen.

I was seriously told to deal with the future. I suppose this is because, as the oldest living American dramaturg, I have a lot of experience of the past. Dream on. Well, then, in the future, I think you should be urged to remind playwrights to be good *story-tellers* – or better still, *story show-ers*. When most of us are asked what a play is about, we do after all still start with the *plot*. Sure there are no new stories, but the old ones still have an infinite variety of new twists.

Further, I would urge you to consider finding in the plays the *actions* which entertain. I remind you (unnecessarily, I am sure) that entertainment is a wide and varied commodity in theatre, but that by and large monologues, barren language, obvious ideas, commonplace passions are just plain (and I mean plain) boring. Sure, the actor can make them alive for the moment, but the action is zilch finally. I do believe that Nazimova, pressed to perform on stage, could bring an audience to tears reciting the Polish alphabet, but that doesn't make the Polish alphabet a theatrical piece or a work of theatrical action.

I urge you, too, to remember the audience (yes, I know I sound like the business office). But the truth is that when we plan, rehearse, present our plays, too often we forget that in order to have theatre we must have an action, actors to perform that action, a place which we accept as magical, and *an audience*. Denigrating the audience, dismissing it as stupid, oafish, provincial, will leave us (my old joke) playing with ourselves. The audience is where it is, and we can move it to new territory, but we need to move it gently and we must move with it, or I fear our theatres will die – perhaps noble deaths but deaths all the same.

I think that theatre people, particularly in these times but perhaps always, need to *hustle* rather than ruminate. We need to be theatrical rather than pedantic, we need to tend the shop rather than try to resolve all the ills in the world. And our shop is the stage, the house of illusions, the brothel of humankind.

I have some specific suggestions which I would like briefly to outline, as I first did some five or six years ago:

First: you – the Literary Managers and Dramaturgs of the Americas here assembled – need to help theatres find competent readers of new plays, to set the standards which a 'literary manager' or a 'dramaturg' needs to bring to the job.

Second: yup, we have to start somewhere, and I think LMDA needs to think through the notion of accrediting both theatre dramaturgs and teachers of dramaturgy. Duschamp's notion that 'Whatever I spit is art' (or whatever he said – no one told me to be accurate) will no longer suffice. I am frightenend at what I hear some literary managers and dramaturgs and teachers talking about. If I may (and try to stop me now), I would insist that all those dramaturgy courses and degrees be grounded in *theatre* rather than in literature.

Third – and here I go again: I think LMDA must lead the way to finding some reliable way of getting rid of most of the scripts which clog our mails and our offices and our desks. The same tired manuscripts wander listlessly from theatre to theatre, and I fear that they only waste our time, our postage, and our patience. *The Script Review* is a beginning, but it is only that.

Although I agree that the worst plays of the lot will finally fall off the circuit, we need for the rest some means of exchanging reactions. I am not sure how to work this, but I think LMDA must devote some of its energy to this, or we will continue to plod through each and every script – and to what purpose? Of course we all will not agree on every play but we certainly will, I hope, agree on the worst ones. And yes, I feel guilty when I don't read the damned play – and even worse when I don't finish it. But I am old now, and I am willing to assume guilt. Anyway, need every script finally be read (competently or not) at every theatre?

And fourthly: some years ago I was advised not to try to write any kind of critique to send to the playwright whose work either I couldn't recommend or which we at the theatre would not be considering for production. A dialogue (in writing) might be useful, but it is again time consuming. So, in all the years that I have conscientiously read plays and written up notes for my own edification and failing memory, I never told a playwright what to do with his/her play, although at times I was tempted. (Read that as you may.)

Interestingly, some writers flatteringly remember how helpful I was, although we didn't do the play: but all I ever said was either 'Let's see your next play, please', or 'I wish I could find a theatre to produce this play.' On the other hand, once my theatre was committed at least to a reading and maybe even a production of a play, I would then (*and only then*) volunteer (and let me stress that word) to help if (and only if) the playwright wanted to know what I had to say. Sometimes they said yes, and sometimes they said no. More often than not they said yes, and then didn't pay much attention to what I had said. That's fine. That's the game we play.

I think some words must be said about the National Endowment for the Arts – not in condemnation or even in pleading for more money (which seems to be what *American Theatre* magazine does to excess), but rather to point out that to succeed, whether as a national funding agency (the NEA) or as theatre, we need clearly to know what we are doing *and why*.

In short, I see the NEA's apparent failure and perhaps demise as a matter of waffling, and I further see some of our theatre's failures and perhaps demise as a matter of waffling as well – of trying to be all things to all people, of not knowing why we are doing plays (rather than delivering lectures or writing diatribes, for example), of not taking a stand and sticking to it. Rather then than damning the NEA, I would suggest that we look to our own houses.

Finally (ah, at last) I would hope that dramaturgs and literary managers might do some of the following things, in their theatres and classrooms as well as in their organization:

• Encourage new writing where talent is perceived, where a voice is heard, or even a 'vision' is glimmering.

• Remember to preserve as best we can the traditions of theatre – and I remind you that I think those traditions are filled with joy and excitement rather than condemnation and gloom.

• Keep constantly in touch with the past so that the wide international heritage is not lost, including the search for plays which must be translated and brought to our audiences because they are theatrically exciting.

• Help to inform the audience when the audience wants to be informed.

• Be ten years ahead of the artistic director in planning future seasons, so there is both rhyme and reason in each clump of seasons, rather than just whim.

• Keep an eye open for acting and directing talent as it grows in the company, and then seek plays to 'stretch' those talents.

• Inform the company of what is going on in other theatres, in the world theatre – in the world, if you will. Report on what other theatres, here and abroad, are doing and why . . . and why this should matter to us.

• Forget about being the intellectual gurus of the company and perhaps rather assume the older, less respectable mantles of magician, charlatan, and (my own favourite) medicine show con man.

In other words, let's start having some fun back stage, in our offices, and on stage. Or in simpler terms still: come off it!

Like Sarah Bernhardt, I seem to have an unending number of Final Farewell Appearances, but let me wish you all well, and hope that you break a leg or two along the way. I thank you very much.

Stacy Wolf

All about Eve: Apple Island and the Fictions of Lesbian Community

We continue our occasional series on the actuality and the ideology of lesbian performance with a study of Apple Island, a performance space in Madison, Wisconsin. Many of the productions of this 'women's cultural and art space' could, suggests Stacy Wolf, be categorized as performance art: she looks at these in the context of other modes and definitions of cultural production, and at the 'complex interplay of identity and knowledge' which constructs Apple Island's potential spectators. Looking at both positive and negative critiques of its work, she concludes that the activity through which its refusal of political and performative divisions is best exemplified is the weekly class-cum-performance of country western line dancing, and suggests through folkloric analogy how this helps to define or redefine the meaning of cultural feminism. Stacy Wolf is a doctoral candidate in Theatre and Drama and a lecturer in Women's Studies at the University of Wisconsin, Madison. She has also published articles in *Theatre Studies*, *Women and Performance*, and the *Journal of Dramatic Theory and Criticism*.

ABOUT A MILE from the capitol building in Madison, Wisconsin, on a major road lined with car dealerships, a lumber yard, Jiffy Lube, and an occasional bar, sits Apple Island, a women's cultural and art space. This location – a fair distance from Madison's theatres and gay bars – works both geographically and metaphorically. Apple Island's brick, industrial, inconspicuous, and virtually unsigned facade requires a knowing spectator even to find the entrance. Its activities and performances inscribe an audience whose spectating practices belie identity politics even as the space tries to institute them.

What I plan to do in this paper is to describe Apple Island as a site of sub-cultural production and to look at the various ways spectators use the place. As one location in Madison where lesbian identities are enacted, Apple Island and the attendant discourses of Madison's women's community construct a notion of lesbian identity through cultural production. I will suggest that these local configurations of lesbian identities and of a lesbian community are useful fictions that both elide difference to maintain their hegemony, and at the same time provide a significant venue for alter-

native cultural production. As Georges Van Den Abbeele notes in his introduction to *Community at Loose Ends*, there is 'an element of demagoguery or mystification at work in the seductive appeal to community'.[1] Like him, my intent is to analyze critically and specifically that mystifying element to 'develop a more just logic of community'.[2]

Apple Island opened two years ago in a refurbished warehouse. From the outside, it is marked by a very small sign with its logo – an apple on a wave, suggestive of nature, movement, and Eve. The image at once reappropriates the symbol of patriarchy's bad girl, the symbol of her desire for knowledge, and links that image to a more traditional female affiliation with water. The logo emblematizes Apple Island's attempt to rework the feminine. The name also emphasizes the idea of a safe and separate space.

There are no numbers at the entrance and, once inside what looks like an office building, no markers or directions to the space itself, which is around the corner, in the back. Like spectators who go to New York's WOW Cafe, you have to know how to get to Apple Island to get there. The teleology of the location refers to a similarly teleological lesbian identity, based on a self-knowledge and self-naming implicated in representation. As Judith Roof points out, 'Identifying as a lesbian already requires a circle where experience and representation define one another.'[3]

Self-Definition of a Women's Community

Although Apple Island advertises some of its events by posting fliers in several local merchants' windows, and by listing them in *Feminist Voices*, a local, bi-weekly newspaper, only three sites provide complete information about the activities: A Room of One's Own, Madison's feminist bookstore which, like Apple Island, constructs itself as a community centre; Sue Goldwoman's weekly radio programme, *Her Turn*, on WORT community radio; and Apple Island itself. While there is public access to information about Apple Island, it clearly functions subculturally through a network of mutually supporting organizations and businesses.

Many of Apple Island's events are fund-raisers – a dance for the local women's transit authority, a performance to raise money for women with disabilities, a concert to send two women to France to study with a political guru. Apple Island's monetary alliance with specific local organizations connects the performative with the political. Its sliding scale fees extend this connection to the personal. In contrast to Madison Civic Center, where art-for-art's-sake amasses the city's cultural capital, or the University Theatre, where art functions pedagogically, Apple Island's performances reinforce the community's sense of its own existence, perpetuating an economic and ideological network.

In order to be able to comprehend much of the publicity, potential spectators need a political and cultural context. While the Civic Center's slick brochures at once invite anyone and promote the sense that Madison is a cultural centre that welcomes touring Broadway shows, Apple Island's publicity produces its own community boundaries.

The flier for Peg's passing, for example – a dance and party that commemorated the anniversary of the death of a local feminist activist – presumes that you know who Peg was. A complex interplay of identity and knowledge construct Apple Island's potential spectators.

Apple Island and its audience participate in a struggle over the meaning of Madison's women's community. While most of the women to whom I've spoken see Apple Island embodying its most vocal and visible contingent, and describe its aesthetic and ideology as cultural feminist, whether these terms carry a positive or negative inflection depends on a spectator's perception of her own insiderness or outsiderness.

Most spectators acknowledge the expectation of insiderness. For some, it's the offer of a safe space; for others, it's an oppressive or exclusionary one. Stephanie, for example, who works at the Women's Studies Research Center and receives monthly fliers from Apple Island, described 'a double message of inclusion-exclusion':

Clearly, if they send fliers to everyone [at Women's Studies] they're trying to be welcoming in some way . . . but the fliers themselves are peculiar in that they carry almost no information unless you already know the language.

She told me that, before our conversation, she could not decipher what Apple Island was:

I knew only that Apple Island was some kind of space where something related to women went on, that I was supposed to be (and wanted to be) interested in but where I knew, vaguely, that I couldn't go. . . . It really seems that their fliers are more anti-publicity than anything else.

Despite or maybe because of Apple Island's exclusions, I am interested in tracking the use value of such a cultural 'community' space for variously positioned spectators. I believe that Apple Island is presently providing a vital and significant cultural space. It is supported and frequented by an active audience community. Naomi, for example, who attends Apple Island regularly and whose friends have performed there, said that the place is welcoming, not exclusionary, and that the surrounding folklore of censorship and of a dogmatic feminist political-correctness is inaccurate.

'Safe Space' and Identity Politics

Over the past year, Apple Island has housed both events and meetings. The events and their publicity fliers can be read intertextually through discourses of cultural feminism, lesbian separatism, and local history and folklore. They illustrate what cultural feminism is made to mean in this space.

Posters are often phrased as invitations, reading 'come join us' or stating that a performer will 'share' her music with us. 'Women' stands as an unproblematized signifier, unmarked by other identity categories. Many of the original performances deal with issues of women's spirituality and women's rituals, like one called *The Joy of Spinning*. Another, called *The Naked Truth*, was both performance art and music, and focused on women's self-empowerment. Virtually all the performances are followed by a dance, which encourages all who attend to become physically and socially active.

A flier advertising a birthday party typifies Apple Island's publicity and how it inscribes a particular audience. Calling the place 'a haven of independence' emphasizes a separatist ideology where women's culture flourishes in isolation. Apple Island, so the poster says, is for women: the event features a women's band, and the grand prize reinforces this circularity by rewarding the winner with one year's admission to Apple Island.

A photograph of potential spectators also encourages a specific spectatorial identification. The four women are fairly clearly, stereotypically marked as lesbians, with short hair, hands in jeans' pockets, androgynous clothing, and a rather defiant but joyful expression. The word 'free' appears three times on the poster – once stating that personal care attendants are admitted free of charge, and twice more in reference to the space being alcohol, smoke, and scent free. What's free at Apple Island is meant, as the poster reads, 'to increase accessibility.'

Because the rhetoric is of accessibility, not of rules or prohibitions, specific spectators – women with disabilities, women who don't smoke, drink, or wear scented products – are encouraged to attend. While I completely support increased accessibility, I am troubled by the conflation of smoking and drinking with the wearing of perfume and physical disabilities.

Apple Island's insistence on creating a safe space perpetuates the false ideal that there can be a safe space. Sociologist Iris Marion Young has analyzed the connection between feminism's quest for a romanticized safe space, and the debilitating assumptions of identity politics that coalesce in such a desire for community.[4] Explicitly, insiderness at Apple Island seems to depend on knowledge and on the ability to read the signs of the publicity and the performances. Implicitly, however, this knowledge relies on identity politics.

Many cultural theorists have launched critiques of identity politics, arguing that it relies on essentialist notions of identity. Visibility is predicated on labelling, which is predicated on self-knowledge, supporting an overly coherent and rigid concept of identity, and, as Diana Fuss notes, an overly coherent and rigid concept of politics.[5] Judith Butler, for example, urges the end of naming lesbian identity as such. She argues that in order to come out of the closet as a lesbian, one must perpetually recreate the closet: that is, by naming one's identity as 'lesbian' one judges and condemns others who are lesbian but who just haven't said it.[6]

What is interesting about the use of identity politics at Apple Island is that it seems to work on a level more connotative than denotative. The word 'lesbian' almost never appears on publicity, and I don't think I have ever heard the word spoken in the place (the closest would be a singer who talked about 'coming out' and 'loving women', but she never used the word 'lesbian'). 'Womon' (with an 'o') and 'womyn' (with a 'y') signify the intended community, specifically sexed and politicized. The identity politics of Apple Island are prevalent, definitive, and unspoken, but subtextually speak what Jean-Luc Nancy calls 'the myth of their own community', which Young describes as an ideal, utopian, ultimately stultifying imperative.[7]

Feminism as Cultural Production

Many spectators' comments and many of my own experiences at Apple Island bear out these critiques. Cathy, for example, commented that, at one concert, she resented being told by the performers what the songs were about and how to interpret them. She felt her autonomy and agency as a spectator denied. As a Bakhtinian spectator, she wanted to provide her own accent on terms like 'oppression' and 'patriarchy'. In Apple Island's context, the terms functioned monologically, as unmoveable signifiers. At the same concert and in a similar Bakhtinian vein, Martha explained that she didn't feel she could make jokes or be parodic there.[8]

It would be easy to dismiss Apple Island as naive, essentialist, and dogmatic, as many potential spectators do on the basis of these complaints. But I want to follow Katie King's suggestion to complicate 'cultural feminism' – to read it in terms of women's cultural production rather than continually to conflate it with the anti-pornography movement.[9] I would like to take up Teresa de Lauretis's call to specify the actions in a feminist community, to redraw 'community' as a productive site.[10]

Another poster, for example, belies a singular notion of lesbian identity by imaging two completely different lesbian styles. The spelling of 'womyn' and the picture of Judy Fjell both signify cultural feminism. She appears in a spiked haircut and upturned collar with acoustic guitar, and played at the Michigan Womyn's Music Festival (which recently decided to admit only 'women born women'). But the 'Girls in the Nose' occupy a parodic mode, reappropriating the label 'girl', wearing dark lipstick, seductive sequined halter tops, and loving the camera in a competely different tone than the women on the party poster.

Whatever our perceived location in the lesbian style wars or in Apple Island's inside-outside dichotomy, as spectators we still make various uses of Apple Island's discourses, practising what Michel de Certeau calls poaching.[11] De Certeau argues that readers do not absorb a text in its entirety, but rather pick and choose what to take in and what to ignore. For de Certeau, the critic should not ask what a text is about, but rather analyze various readings of a text to illuminate underlying assumptions about specific positionalities and reading practices. In this way, consumption of a text is theorized as the production of meaning, positing an active, invested reader rather than a cultural dupe.

I would suggest that a rather differently articulated spectatorial poaching operates in a location like Apple Island, which is circumscribed by a community imperative. Even as spectators seem to be merely describing Apple Island or its productions or events, they are already interpreting, already actively reading, already reworking the meaning of 'women's community' and, by extension, 'cultural feminism'.

Louise, for example, who has been both a performer and a spectator at Apple Island, feels that she cannot be included in Apple Island's community because she doesn't sleep with women, even though she does identify herself as a 'political lesbian.' Louise's comments are significant because they clarify a nuanced identity that some critiques of cultural feminism may elide: that is, while cultural feminism is often accused of being anti-sex, Louise sees Apple Island as being precisely about sex. Louise would say that she is describing the community and its boundaries, but I would suggest she is very actively poaching community iconography.

Class, Dance, Performance

Perhaps the activity that best exemplifies Apple Island's refusal of political and performative divisions is country western line dancing, an extremely popular weekly activity. Participating in country western line dancing forced me to reconsider what

31

I meant by describing Apple Island as 'cultural feminist,' and how I imagined community boundaries.

Not simply a class or a dance or a performance or an easy way to pick someone up, country western line dancing is all of these. Many women at the bi-weekly event know each other and know the instructors, blurring the distinction between the performers and audience. Because everyone dances and because Apple Island is a place where lesbians can perform our sexuality overtly, everyone becomes an actor. Country western line dancing functions as what folklorist Roger D. Abrahams calls a 'display event' – the public world of a subculture, performing for itself its 'technique of bonding and boundary-making'.[12]

While the physicality of the dancing suggests a lesbian identity which is jaunty, blue-jeaned, and a bit sweaty, the language of the teacher-leaders indicates the specific discursive construction of lesbian identity through a number of assumptions and in-jokes. For example, Katie and Laura apologize at the beginning that a few of the songs will contain masculine pronouns. They mention in passing that they learned country western line dancing 'at Michigan'. They move through the dances very slowly, stressing that 'There are no mistakes, just variations.'

During the evening, there is both an insistence to find a mate, to be coupled, and a constant reminder that 'no partners [are] necessary'. The dances are learned individually, but an easy variation makes it into a couple dance. Also the turns and crosses of many of the dances put bodies in close proximity to one another. The leaders constantly make sexual jokes and comments – for example, 'You'll like this part because you can look at how tight her jeans are', or 'This is the part where you can give her a little wink or a smile.'

As an active, embodied activity, country western line dancing requires both disciplining the body and making it a spectacle for female consumption. K. D. Lang, who recently officially came out as a lesbian, serves as the idolized spectre – bold, brazen, and inimitably sexual – as well as a referent to mainstream fashion which increasingly incorporates a historically lesbian style. Country western line dancing refuses easy dichotomies of lesbian identity and style. Neither Birkenstocked, flannel-shirted separatists nor lipstick lesbians, country western line dancing in Madison reconfigures cultural feminism in a rhetoric that is both sexualized and politically correct.

As a structured, sequential activity, country western line dancing is seductive, encouraging insiderness in a space that might otherwise exclude the very same spectators – me, for example. I would suggest, though, that looking at specific activities and employing methodologies which analyze spectators' use of the space can trouble a monolithic notion of cultural feminism, to refine and repoliticize it through cultural practices.

Notes and References

1. Georges Van Den Abbeele, 'Introduction', in *Community at Loose Ends*, ed. Miami Theory Collective (Minneapolis: University of Minnesota Press, 1991), p. ix.

2. Ibid., p. ix.

3. Judith Roof, *The Lure of Knowledge* (New York: Columbia University Press, 1992), p. 120.

4. See Iris Marion Young, 'The Ideal of Community and the Politics of Difference,' in *Feminism/Postmodernism*, ed. Linda J. Nicholson (New York; London: Routledge, 1990), p. 300-23.

5. See Diana Fuss, *Essentially Speaking* (New York; London: Routledge, 1989).

6. Judith Butler, 'Imitation and Gender Insubordination', in *Inside/Out: Lesbian Theories, Gay Theories*, ed. Diana Fuss (New York; London: Routledge, 1991), p. 13-31.

7. Quoted in Van Den Abbeele, op. cit., p. xv.

8. See M. M. Bakhtin, *Speech Genres and Other Late Essays* (Austin: University of Texas Press, 1986).

9. Katie King, 'Producing Sex, Theory, and Culture', in *Conflicts in Feminism*, ed. Marianne Hirsch and Evelyn Fox Keller (New York; London: Routledge, 1990), p. 82-101.

10. Teresa De Lauretis, 'The Essence of the Triangle or, Taking the Risk of Essentialism Seriously: Feminist Theory in Italy, the US, and Britain', *Differences*, I, No. 2 (Summer 1989), p. 3-37.

11. Michel De Certeau, *The Practice of Everyday Life*, trans. Steven Rendall (Berkeley: University of California Press, 1984).

12. Roger D. Abrahams, 'Shouting Match at the Border: the Folklore of Display Events', in *And Other Neighborly Names*, ed. Richard Bauman and Roger D. Abrahams (Austin: University of Texas Press, 1981), p. 305.

James Ross Moore

The Gershwins in Britain

Overwhelmingly, the British reputation of George Gershwin is as a 'serious' composer: but this is liable to obscure not only the contributions he and his brother Ira made to the popular music theatre in Britain, but also, conversely, the British influences upon this seemingly all-American pair. George was profoundly influenced by that pre-eminent American Anglophile of his time, Jerome Kern, while British influences upon the semi-scholarly Ira extended far beyond W. S. Gilbert and P. G. Wodehouse. After 'Swanee' swept Britain in 1920, and George had honed his art and craft by writing the score for the West End revue, *The Rainbow* (1923), came the musical comedy, *Primrose* (1924) – its score his first to be published, and including some of his earliest orchestrations. A prototype of the frivolous comedies of the era, *Primrose* marked the first time the brothers were billed together as the Gershwins, since Ira had earlier written as 'Arthur Francis': it was also the immediate precursor of their first great Broadway hit, *Lady, Be Good!* Finally, in 1928, Ira collaborated, without George, on the London show *That's a Good Girl* – though *Damsel in Distress*, the brothers' last film musical, was a valedictory to the British-American musical comedy of the era. James Moore's earlier transatlantic study, of Cole Porter in Britain, appeared in NTQ30 (1992), and his Radio Two programme on the revue producer André Charlot was broadcast in October 1993.

WRITING after the London opening of *Funny Face* in 1928, a *Tatler* journalist lauded the 'comic caper of Miss Adele Astaire, who is too cute for words, and the dancing of this unique little person with her loose limbed brother Fred, who has invented endless new steps of bewildering intricacy.' He added: 'Mr. Gerschwin's music is up to all the rhythmic dodges which enslave the modern ear. His sister's lyrics are neat and nippy.'

Sic! Never mind. Between 1920 and 1928, George and Ira Gershwin were significant contributors, jointly and separately, to the British musical stage. Aside from inter-polations and transferred Broadway shows, they wrote three full-length original scores for the British musical stage. It is now clear enough that these ventures mark an important stage in George and Ira's compositional and lyric-writing skills. And during this time the Gershwins cut a typical cross-section of the most exciting and expansive years in the first golden age of the British-American musical. None of these aspects has received sufficient attention.

How sad, especially for Ira. Ira Gershwin was a nearly complete Anglophile, second

to none in his Savoyardist generation in the tribe of W. S. Gilbert, second to none as devotee and student of P. G. Wodehouse – and, ultimately, second to none as PGW's competitor and rival. The impassioned yet ironic heart of Ira is visible in a famed lyric he wrote for the film of Wodehouse's *Damsel in Distress*. How incredibly sad: the British Museum has lost its charm! It was Ira who rewrote Congreve, an author not cherished by Tin Pan Alley, as follows: 'Not only hath music charms to soothe the sav-age breast/To soften rocks, undo the clen-ched fist . . . /It refurbisheth the puissance the cliché once possessed./(How fortunate the priv'leged lyricist!')

Perhaps Ira's sheer devotion is seen as effrontery, especially since he eventually proved able to write in truly Gilbertian terms and forms. Yet it is brother George, a man who cheerfully incorporated whatever musical influences his environment sent his way, who became a British icon – as per-manent as Glenn Miller. In *The Oxford Companion to Music*, he is the only twentieth-century American pop composer to rate his own entry, and a national newspaper

33

recently exalted him over Copland, Ives, Still, and Schuman. When George died in 1937, one obituarist noted that Chopin had also died at 39. Fifty years later he was regularly acclaimed as 'the modern Mozart'.

George's supreme accolade – making the top twenty in fifty years of *Desert Island Discs* – helps put things in perspective. It was *Rhapsody in Blue* (and to a lesser degree, *Concerto in F*) that mattered to the reputation, not George and Ira's snappy-smooth ballads.

Even George had to wait for such critical acclaim. His earlier, 'lesser' work – for the musical stage – was a popular success in Britain as early as 1920, but until *Rhapsody* the critics often were not moved. Thus the fortunate historian of musical theatre can cheerfully set aside those 'serious' works. Here follows an examination of the light musical theatre George and Ira Gershwin created for and because of Britain.

The Ubiquity of 'Swanee'

Ira's brother was not dependent for his British influences upon the recordings of Gilbert and Sullivan in their New York dwelling. George fell in love at an impressionable age with the melodic lines of the pre-eminent American Anglophile of his profession. As a legendary rehearsal pianist, he had worked awhile in the mid-1910s at New York's Princess Theatre (where he was also influenced by Guy Bolton and Wodehouse, librettists-lyricists extraordinaire, and passed what he learned on to his brother). He said of his idol, the Princess's composer, 'Jerome Kern was the first composer who made me conscious that most popular music was of inferior quality and that musical comedy music was made of better material. I followed Kern's work and studied each song that he composed.'

The exact beginning of this love-match has been recorded. George was so taken by a tune he heard the orchestra playing at his sister's wedding that he rushed up to the leader to find out what it was. It was Kern's 'You're Here and I'm Here'. He returned shortly for 'They Didn't Believe Me.' Both

were 1914 Kern interpolations into *The Girl from Utah*, a Gaiety musical comedy which wowed Broadway.

It was therefore flattering, fitting, and ironic when Britain set out the red carpet for the 22-year-old George in 1921. In January of that year a newspaper wrote of 'Swanee', an interpolation into Albert de Courville's 1920 revue *Jig Saw*, 'It is the rage of London. You can't get away from it. Every night, everywhere, "Swanee" has been played for months and months with no sign of exhausting its popularity. And London keeps dancing to it.'

The royalties on 'Swanee' bought George a new Steinway grand. Of his welcome at Southampton Gershwin said, 'I felt I was Kern or somebody.' But to the war-weary, dancing-crazed British he had become the epitome of American jazz and 'Swanee' led to Gershwin's first original British score. Yet of all George's popular works, 'Swanee' has always seemed least Gershwinesque – a shameless vehicle for big belters from Jolson through Garland.

It was only one in a decade's worth of pseudo-Southern ditties penned by opportunistic New Yorkers. Its lyricist, the pragmatic Irving Caesar (at this time Ira was still 'Arthur Francis' and very much the junior partner), said he had suggested writing a follow-up to the current one-step hit 'Hindustan', so 'Swanee' was constructed to take advantage of two trends. And if Irving Berlin had earlier swiped a bit of 'Swanee River' to help out 'Alexander's Ragtime Band', so much the better. Add George's evocation of a driving locomotive: there stood 'Swanee,' the compleat Tin Pan Alley production.

Played by George to entertain the girls at a rehearsal of a 1919 Ziegfeld *Frolic* on the New Amsterdam Roof, 'Swanee' caught the particular attention of Ned Wayburn; and therein lies a British-American tale, for Wayburn was a peripatetic of the transatlantic musical, from the 1890s onward a choreographer, director, and free-swinging inventor. He claimed that his 1904 'Syncopated Sandy' was 'the first ragtime theatrical song.' An Italian musical encyclopedia still credits Wayburn with inventing the tap-dance.

In London he had already choreographed several shows, including *Hullo, Ragtime* for Albert de Courville in 1912. De Courville later wrote that Wayburn, working with a megaphone and shouting orders to chorines used to doing no more than nodding in tempo, convinced him that American dance directors were really drill sergeants. In 1919 he was directing a new revue for the new Capitol, the 'world's largest theatre'.

Eventually sixty girls danced for Wayburn to 'Swanee' with electric lights in their shoes. But although the number was well-received, the song didn't sprout wings until Al Jolson made it his own in *Sinbad*. (In those days, songs went where they were wanted.) Suddenly Gershwin was a name. The single song outweighed George's first full-scale show, *La La Lucille*, produced in the same year by Alex Aarons.

The Aftermath of War

Largely on the strength of 'Swanee' (uncredited to Gershwin in the programme, it was the rage of *Jig Saw*, and was recorded by the London Revue Band in June 1920), George eventually received a commission ($1500 and his return fare, plus royalties from any published songs) to write the entire score of a British revue. Its producer would be Albert de Courville, who had accurately judged London's susceptibility to ragtime and would now import 'jazz'.

But first, back to New York and brother Ira went George Gershwin, a man of many projects. In George's absence, 'Arthur Francis' had written songs with Vincent Youmans for *Piccadilly to Broadway*, even though he'd never yet been near Piccadilly. To an English playwright, Paul Potter, is attributed some good advice given Ira at a crucial time. Working days at a Turkish bath and trying at night to write lyrics and items for witty magazines (rather like another Gilbert-worshipper, his college-mate Yip Harburg), Ira met Potter, the dramatist of *Trilby*, who was living upstairs from the baths.

Potter directed Ira to send his satirical paragraphs to H. L. Mencken's *Smart Set*. More importantly, Potter, immersed in the exoticism and energy of American slang, saw that Ira could use it in a graceful and witty way. Write what you know: many an author has profited from such advice. Ira began to wed wisecrackiness to Gilbertism, ultimately achieving an original voice rivalled only by Larry Hart, also of the tribe of WSG.

The triumph of 'Swanee' was one aspect of the tumultuous American theatrical invasion of London after the First World War. The vogue for French adaptations had waned, and the war had enervated all British musical theatre, though revue somehow continued to thrive. Kern, with nearly two decades' lead time, was naturally first among the invaders, contributing two original book musicals. But now American songs, Gershwin's included, became regularly interpolated into London shows.

In 1922, C. B. Cochran's *Mayfair and Montmartre* at the New Oxford – which featured several original songs by Cole Porter, and also Irving Berlin's 'Say It With Music' – incorporated two of George's, with lyrics by Arthur Jackson: these were 'My Lady' and 'South Sea Isles'. The latter featured Nellie Taylor singing, Anita Elson and Joyce Barbour dancing, and a chorus which was as hula-like as London could make it, all set about with Cochran's best palm trees. Cochran was only one producer clamouring for George Gershwin. In less than a year there would be a virtual London Gershwin industry.

Back in New York, George again encountered Fred and Adele Astaire, a team he had met in his days as a rehearsal pianist. Then, he had insouciantly promised them a Gershwin musical of their own. In 1922 George and Arthur's 'Tra La La', a lilting, playfully Germanic love song, was interpolated into Fred and Adele's first New York starring vehicle, *For Goodness' Sake*.

The fabled intertwining of Gershwins and the Astaires ('They dance naturally to the music he writes') brought to the Gershwins another heavily British-American influence.

The Astaires had already learned a lot from Vernon and Irene Castle – he British and she quite American. The Astaires saw the Castles in *The Sunshine Girl* nine times. Undisputed creators of the dancing craze, the Castles brought to Americans an awareness of their own 'democratic right to elegance and the pursuit of fun'. Fred and Adele were the inheritors.

The youthful Noël Coward, exuberant at discovering in his first visit to New York that Americans took light music seriously, went backstage after *The Love Letter* to tell Fred and Adele that they should hurry on over. 'You've got youth, energy, humour, looks, and fun. That's exactly what the English like.'

For Goodness' Sake began in a small way the Gershwin-Astaire collaboration and eventually provided their producers. Its male lead was a young American actor named Vinton Freedley, who, through the Astaires, met the stagestruck part-owner of Finchley's, a New York tie shop. This was Alex Aarons, as we have seen already George's first producer.

When *For Goodness' Sake*, renamed *Stop Flirting*, arrived in Britain for its pre-London run in 1923, it set up a collision. George had written his revue score for de Courville: *The Rainbow* was set to open. George Gershwin would be competing with himself, not for the last time.

De Courville and 'The Rainbow'

De Courville, the reigning king of the gigantic musical (one featured a chorus of 300 and an onstage Niagara Falls) had been importing syncopated American talent for a decade. He was fiercely competitive, as his 1912 feat of luring actress-singer Shirley Kellogg from under André Charlot's nose in New York attests. He went so far as to marry Kellogg, and for a decade his revues were built around her. Part of one sketch by Ronald Jeans from Charlot's most popular revue *Buzz Buzz* (1918-1920), which 'took off' various producers, suggests de Courville's method:

They'll do it at the Hippodrome/In quite a different way./Well, RATHER I should say!/ They'll treat it good and gay!/I guess they'll introduce 'effects'/That fairly swamp the play/ De Courville stuff,/All blare and bluff/Hip-Hippodrome – Hooray!/(I guess they'll pelt the stalls/with real billiard balls!

The star of *Buzz Buzz*, Nelson 'Bunch' Keys, then impersonated Kellogg.

George Gershwin was de Courville's latest American songwriting acquisition. An ex-journalist whose life was changed by seeing the original *Ziegfeld Follies*, de Courville had probably come to regard himself as the British Ziegfeld. He had already employed one of Ziegfeld's favourite ragtime composers, Louis Achille Hirsch, as well as the free spirit Melville Gideon (whose British-American story was told as part of my NTQ article in 1992 on Cole Porter's British career). De Courville was still active in the British-American musical in 1948, when he produced *Lute Song* in London.

For *The Rainbow*, as de Courville's 'eleventh Hippodrome Revue' came to be called, George was partnered by Clifford Grey, a lyricist with impeccable Anglo-American credentials who had collaborated with such British-Americans as Kern and Nat Ayer as well as most of the Tin Pan Alley regulars. Edgar Wallace, a friend of de Courville's and a man whose credits suggested that he believed he could write anything from detective thrillers to imperial panegyrics, collaborated with de Courville on the book.

The Rainbow opened on 3 April 1923, and by the standards of the time and against the prevailing competition, it was no disaster, even though it achieved 'only' 113 performances. The West End musical competition in 1923 was remarkably stiff. Just before *The Rainbow*, Charlot had opened one of his best revues, *Rats*, a star vehicle for the young Gertrude Lawrence, who was termed 'dashing, full of assurance, freely expressing humour from every limb and feature.' And while *The Rainbow* continued, Irving Berlin's *Music Box Revue* showed up. Further competition – both potent and ironic, as we shall see – came over from America in the form of *Stop Flirting* and *Dover Street to Dixie*. After that came Noël Coward's first revue, Charlot's *London Calling*, but by that time *The Rainbow* had disappeared over the horizon.

Dressed in pastels, and, in the mode of the times, sprawling over nineteen scenes, *The Rainbow* was a typical de Courville revue, designed to hook the West End audience on American jazz while upsetting its conventional expectations as little as possible. It featured Lola Raine, Alec Kellaway, Geo Willie, Billy West, Frank McGinty, Grace Hayes, Earl Rickards, Gaston and Andree, the Fayre Four, Ted Thesiger, Stephanie Stephens, Clifford Cobbe, Elaine Lettor, Elsie Mayfair, Fred Leslie, Jack Edge and The Sixteen Empire Girls – and one big surprise. This is how the first two-thirds of the programme went:

1. The Old and New Empire
2. Doctors in 1973
3. Sweethearts (*a chorus and the Sixteen Empire Girls*)
4. My Lady's Boudoir
5. The Price of True Love
6. 'Any Little Time' by Gershwin (*Leslie and chorus*)
7. The Housing Problem
8. 'Midnight Blues' by Gershwin (*Raine and the Sixteen Empire Girls*)
9. A New Style in Songs (*Rickards*)
10. In Old Versailles (*including Gershwin's 'Moonlight in Versailles'*)

Interval

11. On the Embankment (*Gershwin's 'In the Rain'*)
12. Pharoah Among the Ruins
13. Gershwin's 'Innocent, Lonesome Blue Baby' (*Stephens, Kellaway, Ted Grant, and Frances Wing*)
14. Indo China (*notable because all the royals came to see Elaine Howlett in it, her father being in charge of HM wardrobe. It included Gershwin's 'Beneath the Eastern Moon'*)
15. Grace Hayes

At this point an entirely separate show erupted. Item 16 was 'Plantation Days' – '32 coloured singers, dancers, and musicians from the Southern States of America.' These were 'James P. Johnson and his syncopated orchestra and entertainment company' –

Johnson being credited with all the original music – plus these specialities:

Harper and Blanks and Pepper Chorus: simply full of jazz
Four Cracker Jacks: ragtime jubilee
Silver Tone Four: bit of harmonizing
'Previous': Geo Stamper
Plantation Days: Stamper, Josephine Stevens, and entire company

Following 'Plantation Days', *The Rainbow* proper resumed with

17. 'Oh, Nina' by Gershwin
18. All Correct
19. The finale: 'Scarlet and Gold': the Great Strut, featuring Gershwin's 'Strut, Lady with Me' (*Hayes, Leslie, Grant, and Wing*)

These sketches also contained 'Good-night My Dear', 'Sunday in London Town', and 'Sweetheart I'm so Glad that I Met You'. Gershwin's score has been called 'pedestrian and perfunctory', and few traces of it ever reappeared in other Gershwin works.

Despite the innovation of a Gershwin score, *The Rainbow*'s biggest draw was the Plantation Days troupe. Britain had been rather hospitable to American black musical theatre, real and not-so, since minstrel times, and in 1923 there were probably many who remembered the sensation caused by *In Dahomey* ('Real coon dancing by real coons') when it cakewalked over from Broadway twenty years earlier.

Charlot, senses well attuned to the next sensation, had thought the West End ready for a black revival in 1919, when he brought Will Marion Cook's 'Southern Syncopated Orchestra' to the Philharmonic Hall. After all, Cook had written *In Dahomey*. But in the 1950s, reflecting on his career, Charlot labelled the engagement 'a venture ahead of its time'. In 1923 – and it must be said, after 'Swanee' – other producers saw that the time was right for alternate types of 'jazz'.

The Rainbow's opening night programme apologised that the 'varied programme of Plantation Days' is not possible in *The Rainbow*'. A week later the Plantation Days company began an entire show of their own at 5.15 and 11.15 each evening, sandwiching the main offering.

Contemporary reviewers were generally bemused. Their attention was best caught by Jack Edge's curtain speech, in which he took great pleasure in lambasting the increasing tide of Americans on the West End stage. Another week on, the Australian Daphne Pollard, one of de Courville's favourite comic performers (who went on to screen fame as a longsuffering wife in the Laurel and Hardy films) joined the cast. The show underwent further tinkering, but it never caught on.

The Astaires and 'Stop Flirting'

The failure of *The Rainbow* to blitz London conceals some retrospective ironies and a truth about the West End's competitiveness. When he left his song-plugging job at Remick's in New York in 1917, George had made friends with Will Vodery, a black composer and arranger who, in time, was to orchestrate the (failed, despite a production by George White) original version of George's one-act opera, *Blue Monday Blues* (later called *135th St*) and arrange music for some of the Gershwins' shows. Vodery even got Gershwin a one-night job playing the piano at Fox's City Theatre.

When Cochran's *Dover Street to Dixie* came along, its own black jazz effectively dissolving *The Rainbow*'s, at its centre was none other than Will Vodery. The amalgamation of disparates in *Dover Street to Dixie* worked much better than *The Rainbow*'s, perhaps because it was containerized: there was a thoroughly British first act, starring Stanley Lupino, but the entire second half was *The Plantation Revue*, starring Florence Mills. Among her triumphs was 'I'm Just Wild about Harry', borrowed successfully from Eubie Blake and Noble Sissle's *Shuffle Along*, in which she had begun her brief and brilliant career. Among others singing to the accompaniment of Vodery's orchestra was Edith Wilson, another Ziegfeld star, while comic Shelton Brooks, an American favourite, did his broad specialties. Cochran's programme added that Vodery's orchestra could be engaged for private parties – from Cochran.

Though Cockie always took the lion's share of credit and even went so far as to claim he had 'discovered' Mills, *The Plantation Revue* was the creation of Lew Leslie – the first of many black American shows he successfully organized and exported. Born in New York in 1922, *The Plantation Revue* was the real thing, after which de Courville's *Plantation Days* seemed an echo. Its appearance in *Dover Street to Dixie* and elsewhere in Europe can be seen as an elaborate out-of-town tryout, and the revue (the detachable British section left behind) eventually returned to the US as part of *Dixie to Broadway*. Leslie became internationally famed for his *Black Birds* revues, which in one way or another gave London two of its most enduring British-American performers, Adelaide Hall and Elisabeth Welch.

So de Courville's (hence Gershwin's) jazz had been one-upped by Cochran's. Meanwhile, *Stop Flirting* conquered Liverpool, Glasgow, and Edinburgh, arriving at the Shaftesbury on 30 May 1923 (about halfway through *The Rainbow*'s run), where it settled for the longest run (418 performances) of any Astaire stage show. Sydney Carroll's review in *The Times* tried to assess the Astaires: 'The tops, with an extraordinary lightness, empathy, and yet as odd as golliwogs.'

To the score of *Stop Flirting*, nominally by William Daly and Paul Lannin, the Gershwins now added 'I'll Build a Stairway to Paradise', lifted from their contributions to the George White *Scandals of 1922*. *Stop Flirting* was produced by one of the British-American musical's key figures, George Grossmith, Jr., who added some of his own numbers. The co-producers were J. A. E. Malone, Alfred Butt (the Unionist MP for Wandsworth, who had been director of rationing during the war), and . . . Alex Aarons.

The Rainbow was also overmatched against Adele. According to *The Sketch*, 'Girls who are tired of shingling and think of growing their hair can study Miss Adele Astaire's picture . . . for two charming and novel notes in long haired coiffures, as both the soft puffs and the demure plaits, or "listening-in-ear-piece" plaits are exceedingly fetching arrangements.'

The Prince of Wales claimed to have seen *Stop Flirting* ten times. James Barrie said he would like to have Adele play *Peter Pan*. (Another American musical star who became a major Gershwin interpreter, Dorothy Dickson, eventually did.) And the Astaires went on to become London semi-regulars, increasingly in the company of Coward and of Gershwin songs. Astaire arranged dances for some of Coward's songs in the smash 1923 Charlot-Coward *London Calling*, and Astaire attended some composition classes at the Guildhall School of Music in 1924 while he was helping Coward with his tap-dancing. He wrote a song with Austin Melford for *The Co-Optimists of 1924*, and his 'Not My Girl', written with Desmond Carter, was briefly popular.

On 11 June 1924, Donald Calthrop's revue *Yoicks!* opened at the Kingsway on Great Queen Street, starring Calthrop, Mary Leigh, Louis Goodrich, Mark Lester, and Richard Dalliman. Coward placed two numbers in this British-American show, 'It's the Peach' and 'I'd Like to See You Try'. The latter was 'arranged by Fred Astaire'– and so was 'By and By,' Gershwin's collaboration with William Daly, A. E. Thomas, and Brian Hooker.

'Primrose' – the Lost Musical

George was in Britain now after the American premiere of *Rhapsody in Blue*, writing (now for Grossmith, who had been rumoured to prefer Kern) his first book musical for the West End. On 8 July he wrote to his friend and collaborator Lou Paley and Paley's wife Em: 'If the show is only half way decent it will be produced in America soon after its London presentation.'

On 11 September 1924, *Primrose* opened at the Winter Garden, where it ran for 255 performances. Heather Thatcher, who had already appeared in Kern shows at the same house, joined a characteristic Winter Garden troupe – Leslie Henson, Vera Lennox, Percy Heming, Claude Hulbert, and Margery

Hicklin – in a show whose importance has been undervalued, especially in Britain, where it is a truly 'lost' musical.

Guy Bolton, the Princess series nominally ended, had contracted with Aarons and Freedley for a show featuring the Astaires, and for one more in Britain after Wodehouse's *The Beauty Prize* (for Kern). This was *Primrose*. In accordance with the practice of the time, Bolton shared his writing credit with Grossmith, who had apparently considered Coward but decided on Bolton's track record.

Bolton and Wodehouse, both singly and together, were nearly as prolific as their highly inventive mid-career collaborative autobiography, *Bring on the Girls*, suggests. Wodehouse was the word-man and Bolton the expert constructionist (those hiring him were taking out play-doctor insurance). Together or apart, they never strayed very far from the plots they had invented for those Princess classics.

The plot of *Primrose* is such a contrivance and typifies the era's musical comedies. It suggests the task set for George, for Ira (finally writing under his own name – there was already a British Arthur Francis), and for Carter, a British lyricist Ira ranked with PGW as Gilbert's authentic heir. Here follows a summary of *Primrose* from *Play Pictorial*, notable for its own lighthearted ennui:

Joan (Hicklin) – charming and inexperienced – lives with her guardian Sir Barnaby Falls (Guy Fane) in his riverain mansion, on one of the upper reaches of the Thames. Just beyond its garden walls, Hilary Vane (Heming), a novelist, has moved his houseboat, *The Wagtail*. He is at work on a serial called *Primrose*, of which Joan is an enthusiastic reader. She assumes she's the model for the title role. They appear to know each other by sight only. Prompted by hero worship, she slips through his garden gate, sees a manuscript, takes a page from it, and is detected by the author. Some serio-comic love interest is added by the sprightly maiden May Rooker (Lennox) and Freddie Falls (Hulbert), the 'up to date' son of Sir Barnaby. There is utter disregard of Barnaby's arranged plan, which is to marry Freddie to Joan.

The comic lovers are Toby Mopham (Henson), scion of an ancient family, and Pinkie Peach

(Thatcher), who is in business as Mme Franz-aline, a beauty specialist from the West End. They had met at a dance; there, under the spell of champagne and her eyes, he proposed and was accepted. Toby has come up the river as Hilary's guest, astonishing him by inviting Pinkie for luncheon, so his friend can write her a good advertising notice. Pinkie arrives with her brother Michael (T. Weguelin), her chauffeur. Pinkie makes very good progress with Hilary. When Joan appears, she's disillusioned. Pinkie faints into Hilary's arms and Toby sees that, too.

At the Hotel Splendide in Le Bouquet, every-one is celebrating 14 July, Bastille Day. Of course, all the characters from Little Ferry-on-Thames are there. Joan pines. She is assisted by her new friend Pinkie. . . . Joan carries on with 'boys' for Pinkie, Hilary now suspects his Primrose is not the unsophisticated flower of his imagination.

Joan consents to marry Freddie. Hilary plots to horrify Barnaby and prevent it. She enlists a professor of spiritualism, Herr Pshoveleski, who cancels his reservation at the last moment. So Toby now impersonates him, horrifying Barnaby with tales of Freddie's nature. It works. Toby continues to impersonate the professor until his mother, Lady Mopham, recognizes him. His disguise is torn by Pinkie, who wasn't in on the joke.

Lady Mopham now converts her town house into a dancing club. Toby reciprocates his mother's actions by becoming a raiding police-man. So Lady Mopham faints into Barnaby's arms. Since all the love interests are satisfied, it is now genuinely Primrose time.

Aside from being the first score upon which the Gershwins collaborated under both their own names, *Primrose* was George's first score to be published in full (by Chappell in London and Harms in New York). Of special musical significance was George's orchestration of three songs – 'Naughty Baby', 'Isn't It Wonderful?', and 'Berkeley Square and Kew'.

The Question of Orchestration

Since *Primrose* came midway between *Rhapsody in Blue* and *Concerto in F* in 1925, these orchestrations are considered to settle a scholarly controversy – when did George learn orchestration? It seems now that he didn't orchestrate *Rhapsody* for the reason he gave: he was too busy. The first of many collaborations between the Gershwins and Bolton, *Primrose* was one of the first London

musicals to be broadcast in part by the BBC. It also marked the first time an English reviewer said Ira was George's sister.

Claiming that in his score for *Primrose*, he had paid particular attention to English phrases and enunciation, George remarked that 6:8 was the tempo best suited to convey in music a mimetic sense of English conversation. And it is often suggested that why *Primrose* never transferred to the USA was because Gershwin had written such a perfectly 'English' score – a myth perpetuated by remarks such as that attributed to Aarons: 'Berkeley Square' (near which the Gershwins, Aarons, and his wife stayed while the show was taking shape) was 'more English than anything Paul Rubens ever wrote'. No English critic noticed this.

Now that the original score of the show has been recovered (part of the celebrated find in a warehouse in Secaucus, New Jersey, in 1982), performed (in Brooklyn) and in 1987 to a degree recorded ('Gershwin Overtures': EMI 27 0575 1) this view should be reconsidered: Gershwin's score was, with exceptions, about as 'English' as Richard Rodgers's for *The King and I* was authentically Siamese. But it is bracing, inventive, and tuneful. Perhaps the greatest significance of *Primrose*, as Edward Jablonski has said, is that it is 'composed-through', musical exposition setting the tone throughout. (Still, it was only three years later that George and Ira produced some deliberately Savoyard numbers for *Strike up the Band*.)

Considering the practices of the time, the score of *Primrose* was startlingly original. Of its nineteen numbers (including an act-opening ballet) George recycled 'American' material in only three. It's true, there was nothing particularly sweet-and-lowdown-jazzy about this score. But in the show's best songs, there is always a point where brisk-ness eases and the melodic line becomes languorously saxophonic: Gershwin songs.

Desmond Carter received more lyric credit than Ira, whose name appeared in the published score six times – once with B. G. DeSylva (for 'Some Far-Away Someone'). Ira's only solo credit was 'Four Little Sirens We', a quartet for the beach scene at Le

Scenes from *Primrose*. Top: Joan (Margery Hicklin) sings 'Isn't It Wonderful?' ('Any man who would appeal to me, / Must appeal in every way'). Bottom: Tony (Leslie Henson) sings 'When Tony Is Out of Town' ('London is a sorrow-ful place, / You'll find a frown on every face, / When Tony is out of town').

Bouquet obviously patterned upon *The Mikado* ('Four little Sirens, we/Making the mermen fall for us/We never go in the sea/But we work as well as any Sirens of mythology'). 'Four Little Sirens We' had found its proper home. As 'The Sirens', it was written by 'Arthur Francis' to his brother's music for *A Dangerous Maid*, which closed in Pittsburgh in May 1921. The onstage Primrose sirens managed the inconsiderable feat of looking vaguely Viking .

Arguably the best, most recognizably Gershwin songs from *Primrose* were those George wrote with Ira. In 'Wait a Bit, Susie', whose catchy melody falls trippingly down the scale, and (in the tradition of the era's 'plug' songs) becomes maddeningly embedded in the brain (a reviewer of the Gershwins' subsequent *Tell Me More* gave 'Susie' a southpaw compliment: 'nothing so easily remembered at first hearing as 'Wait a Bit, Susie'') there is more than a hint of the lyricist shortly to write 'Looking for a Boy' in *Tip-Toes*:

(There is Someone who/Some fine day/Will come and say/He loves you/Somebody who's lonely/Someone who only/Wonders what to do/Watching waiting/Hesitating, too.)

Though such safely saucy boy-girl cuteness was part of the musical comedy template and hardly specific to Ira, another preview of 'Looking for a Boy' can be seen in 'Boy Wanted' ('To have the ghost of a chance/He must be able to dance/The sort of boy wanted/Must have a smile./Boy wanted, lovable style.')

If you change its tempo, 'Naughty Baby' ('Naughty baby, naughty baby who will tease you/I can show the way and know the way to please you') sounds startlingly like 'Somebody Loves Me'. And why not? In the golden years of musical theatre, just because you were writing one score didn't mean you weren't just – writing! The first eight bars of 'Fascinating Rhythm' occurred to George while he worked on *Primrose*.

If George and Ira's songs are the best of *Primrose*, perhaps it is because their particular ability to work together, later celebrated in Ira's *Lyrics On Several Occasions*, was

jelling. Talking of 'A Foggy Day', he recalled: 'All I had to say was "George, how about an Irish verse?" and he sensed instantly the degree of wistful loneliness I meant.' Guessing that their method was synthetic, Ira added, 'When . . . I couldn't recall exactly the start of a particular song I wanted to discuss, I would visualize the vocal line and my forefinger would draw an approximation of its curves in the air. And more often than not he would know the tune I meant.'

According to Britain's advanced practice, some of the songs from *Primrose*, including 'Boy Wanted', 'The Mophams', and 'I Make Hay While the Sun Shines', were recorded by its original stars, Thatcher and Henson. As usual, other recordings were made by the Winter Garden Theatre orchestra and the Mayfair Orchestra. On no recordings was Ira credited.

A footnote to *Primrose* was written in 1960 by the ubiquitous Wodehouse. With characteristic irreverence for tradition, including his own, he rewrote two of Carter's lyrics – 'The Mophams' (now 'The Pophams') and 'When Toby Is Out of Town' (now 'The Twenties Are Here to Stay') so that they could be placed in a Broadway revival – of *Oh, Kay!*

London Awash with Gershwin

By the time *Primrose* closed in 1925, London was awash with Gershwin, although critical acclaim was often withheld. One of his songs from *Little Miss Bluebeard* ('I Won't Say I Will', with 'Arthur Francis' and de Sylva), was warmly roasted ('of scarcely sufficient interest to justify what action there was'), as was just about everything else in this showcase for Irene Bordoni. Ms. Bordoni changed costumes eight times and sang five songs (Irving Berlin and E. Ray Goetz were also victimized), and only Eric Blore's silly-ass Englishman won praise. 'We do not often see a worse play', muttered one stunned reviewer of this show – which like its star had been very popular on Broadway.

It was an obvious coincidence, but while George never wrote another original score

The finale to Act I of *Primrose*. Tony: 'So this is where I find you – my affianced wife – in the arms of this man.'

for London, he did now become a regular visitor. When the stars of *Charlot's Revue*, conquerers of Broadway, were feted, the Gershwins were there, and met Gertrude Lawrence. Within three years they would write two shows for her – one a classic and one a flop.

The Gershwins also now became even more regular participants in the transatlantic musical theatre of the era. Their series of New York successes began in 1924 (directly after Primrose) with *Lady, Be Good!* – their first complete collaboration to be produced on Broadway. Its success, which owed something to the reputations which the Gershwins and the Astaires had brought back from London, marked the first of Aarons's and Freedley's attempts to create a new, Princess Theatre-like series, substituting George for Kern (who no longer wanted to write on 'such a small scale').

Bolton was on hand, writing the book with a 'visitor from England', Fred Thomp-son. The book was called *Black Eyed Susan* until Bolton and Thompson heard one of the songs from the score. It was very likely that Wodehouse would have joined this team, but by now George wanted only Ira to write his songs.

An additional fillip to the 'Englishness' of *Lady, Be Good!* is the celebrated tale of Lady Mountbatten and 'The Man I Love.' The number, which had lured American patron Otto Kahn to invest $10,000 in the show, was dropped from *Lady* in Philadelphia because, said Ira, its 'sweetness and simplicity' caused the show's momentum to flag. The song was published anyhow, and later, in New York, George autographed a copy for Lady Mountbatten, who had her favourite band, the Berkeley Square Orchestra, arrange it. Soon it was played all over London, mostly by ear, and shortly its fame spread to Paris. For the rest of the decade 'The Man I Love' kept getting tossed out of Gershwin shows, but its European popularity crossed to America and eventually it became too well-known to be included in any show.

The Gershwins' London success rolled along. While *Lady* ran long on Broadway, its successor *Tell Me More!* (originally called *My Fair Lady*) eased the Gershwins' pain at the closing of *Primrose* by opening at the same theatre, the Winter Garden, on 26 May 1925. It would run 100 performances in New York (the productions actually overlapped each other) but now, adding for box-office insurance songs with others' lyrics – 'The Love I Never Knew' (Carter) and 'Have You Heard' (Claude Hulbert) – it settled in for a long West End run.

The plot of *Tell Me More!* (by Thompson and William Wells) was less than gossamer and filled with stereotypes ('Did you say "Be more British?" I thought you said Yiddish!'). But it was playful and eccentric, again featuring Henson and Thatcher (a Briton who could play Americans, and who was nearly as standard in British-American productions as Dorothy Dickson). *Tell Me More!* and its sprightly if forgettable tunes became such a hot item that its overture was played to accompany an anniversary production of *Charley's Aunt*.

From then on, the London runs of all Gershwin shows, like all Astaire shows, surpassed their New York figures. And when, on 14 April 1926, *Lady, Be Good!* opened at the Empire, in the spirit of the times George added for London three songs *sans* Ira: 'Something about Love' (Lou Paley), and 'I'd Rather Charleston' and 'Buy a Little Button from Us' (Carter).

Six days after the show's London opening, Fred and Adele recorded most of its score. (The earliest Astaire recordings are from *Stop Flirting*, but no Gershwin songs were included). It is this production's recordings which show us what the Astaire-Gershwin collaboration meant – 'The Half of It Dearie Blues' demonstrating, probably on purpose, what it must have been like to be at a party with Fred and Adele and George. This is one of the earliest attempts to capture a dancer (Fred) on record, and George is unmistakably the pianist. (S. N. Behrman

wrote later that when George played his songs at a party, 'The room became freshly oxygenated.') These recordings are included in *The Golden Age of Fred Astaire, Volume Two* (EMI GX41 2538 1).

Lady, Be Good! waited many years for a London revival. In the later 1980s, London's Guildhall School turned out a lovely, peppy, and bright version, perfectly authentic, following it with an equally polished *Girl Crazy*.

On 'Tip-Toes'

The 'syncopated' Gershwin juggernaut rolled over London. *Rhapsody in Blue*, now done as a classic ballet starring Anton Dolin, was performed in *Midnight Follies* at the Hotel Metropole. And Ira married Leonore Strunsky, the sister of Emily Paley, settling down, as he later wrote, to a lifetime of tomayto-tomahto skirmishing. Lee's pronunciation was apparently as elevated as was Ira's booklearning.

On 31 August 1926, *Tip-Toes* opened, once again at the Winter Garden. One of the less ecstatic reviews noted: '*Tip-Toes* is one of the most satisfactory musical comedies seen in London since *No, No, Nanette* was produced nearly eighteen months ago', and *The Times* thought it was simply 'the best musical comedy since *The Belle of New York*'. What sort of West End competition surrounded *Tip-Toes*? Only *Black Birds*, *Sunny*, *Rose Marie*, *The Co-Optimists*, *The Charlot Show of 1926* – and *Lady, Be Good!* London loved *Tip-Toes* – and so has everyone who has written about it since, which is a good enough reason for including it in this study. So is the fact that, because of lagging American practice, our only direct contact with the show is the London cast's recordings.

Exactly why *Tip-Toes* languished more or less forgotten for more than a half-century is a question suitable for treatment elsewhere. The score is as rangy as anything George had produced, the lyrics as lively as any of Ira's. The Bolton and Thompson plot involves an on-their-uppers dance trio (Tip-Toes Kaye is its youthful girl star), a vulnerably wealthy American 'glue king', the inevitable falling-in-love, nearly inevitable amnesia, and the mandatory triumph of true love.

The show is full of blazers, plus-fours, short dresses, and pep. It has been called by musicologists like John McGlinn the epitome of the 'twenties. A stageful of jazzing trombonists lifts the pulse-beat notably. (The opening night programme contains a serious discussion by a Harley Street doctor, who happily concluded that the Charleston is good exercise.)

From the American cast, Allen Kearns (the glue king) was joined by Laddie Cliff ('he has learned to say Ye-ah like an American'), John Kirby, Vera Bryer (on Broadway, this part was Jeanette Mac-Donald's), Evan Thomas, and 'bright-eyed dancing charmer Dorothy Dickson'. Dickson and her husband Carl Hyson had come to London in 1920 after a brief, Castles-like career in the American mid-west and on Broadway. They remained, and Miss Dickson became one of the great stars of the British-American stage. She was Kern's Sally and Rodgers and Hart's Peggy-Ann. For Charlot she sang 'A Cup of Coffee, a Sandwich, and You'. She was Peter Pan, and twice she was an Ivor Novello heroine. Dancing with Walter Crisham, she introduced 'These Foolish Things'.

The London recordings of *Tip-Toes* are joyous: fortunately, they remain available on an LP with the London production of Youmans' *Wildflower* (Monmouth-Evergreen ME5 7052). Ira was happy about *Tip-Toes*. Pleased with *Lady, Be Good!* he realized it contained no comic number. In *Tip-Toes*, the developing artist credited himself with writing longer openings, crisper lines – the first-act finale actually carried plot action for four or five minutes:

I liked the trio 'These Charming People' (in which the Kayes parody the uppity people they believe they are about to meet) which seemed to amuse the audience. Up to then I'd often wondered if I could do a comedy trio like the ones P. G. Wodehouse came up with.

Addressing the question of which came first, the music or the lyrics, in the show's hit,

'That Certain Feeling', Ira gave full vent to his British erudition:

With the great art-song writers of the Elizabethan age (John Dowland, Thomas Campion, and half a dozen others) the words always came first . . . [but] the practice of putting new words to pre-existent song became more and more common and led to the beginnings of ballad opera. England's outstanding opus in this realm was Gay's *The Beggars Opera*, 1728. This was so successful that it ran 62 nights, a new theatrical record that stood unchallenged for almost a century. In the Heinemann edition (London, 1921) I count 68 short 'airs' chosen by Gay from the great store of English, Irish, and Scottish melodies – newly lyricized by the playwright. . . .

Everyone knows that in the Gilbert and Sullivan operettas practically all the lyrics were written first. However, earlier in Gilbert's theatrical career he'd also had plenty of experience setting words to music. In the 1860s he produced in London many extravaganzas and burlesques, based on continental operas. These were adapted by him into English with tricky lyrics and recitatives loaded with puns. Among them were Meyerbeer's *Robert le Diable* which became *Robert the Devil; or the Nun, the Dun, and the Son of a Gun*, and Bellini's *Norma*, extravagandized to *The Pretty Druidess; or the Mother, the Maid, and the Mistletoe Bough*.'

Surely, such a love should have been a bit more requited.

The End of the Affair

While in London early in 1926, the Gershwins re-encountered Gertrude Lawrence – whom their *Oh, Kay!* was shortly to turn into a permanent American star. During the run-up to opening, Ira became ill and it became necessary to ask for lyric help. George again rejected the idea of Wodehouse, who had collaborated on the book, as lyricist, so Howard Dietz contributed some ideas and words. *Oh, Kay!* opened in London on 21 September 1927 at His Majesty's and repeated its success.

In 1927 the Gershwin-Astaire 'team' was involved in a spectacular revue inelegantly called *Shake Your Feet*, which opened at the vast Hippodrome and after 201 performances transferred to the vast Palladium. Gershwin songs were heard in a first-act medley featuring Gwen Farrar and Billy Mayerl, and in the second half a huge production number, a complex tap routine for 36 chorines called 'Tappin' the Time', was written by Astaire with lyrics by Jim Altemus. Anticipating Busby Berkeley, there were five white grand pianos on stage at one time.

The last Astaire-Gershwin collaboration began its final run on 8 November 1928, when *Funny Face* opened at the Prince's. George travelled to London, where he served as a reserve rehearsal pianist. Henson and Sydney Howard were added for the British production. *Funny Face* played until January 1930, during which time *The Tatler* learned Ira's sex and Adele in true musical comedy fashion met her future husband, Lord Charles Cavendish, younger son of the Duke of Devonshire.

Ira Gershwin continued to pursue other collaborations at home and abroad, as did his brother. In 1928 Ira, Phil Charig, Joe Meyer, and Briton Douglas Furber inherited a show which Kern and Oscar Hammerstein II had intended to write. This original for London was *That's a Good Girl*.

Charig had become another of the British-American musical's regulars. A slightly younger friend of the Gershwins (born in 1902), he entered the family circle through George and Ira's brother Arthur. He was a vaudeville pianist for Louise Dresser and others, and in turn became the Gershwins' rehearsal pianist and from 1920 a songwriter. He contributed songs to half a dozen British musicals in the 'twenties and 'thirties (*Lady Mary* perhaps his most successful), as did Meyer, another of the Gershwins' Tin Pan Alley friends.

In 1928 at a special Gershwin evening at London's Kit Kat Club, Charig introduced George to Oscar Levant, and it was Levant who most frequently carried the American banner of Gershwinolatry during the two decades following George's death, right on into the film of *An American in Paris* and countless concerts. Charig's one major success on Broadway was *Follow the Girls* in 1944.

That's a Good Girl was a resounding West End hit – a star vehicle for a reigning British musical comedy team, Elsie Randolph and Jack Buchanan, though the eight smartly drilled Tiller Girls commanded their own share of attention. There were orchestrations by Russell Bennett and a plot about a lady detective, a young man with debts, his operatic friends, and his rich aunt on the Riviera, decorated with plenty of silk-fringed bathing beauties.

With Charig, Ira wrote two songs for Buchanan, 'Whoopee' and 'Let Yourself Go' (neither of these the ones you're thinking of), 'Sweet So and So' for Buchanan and the chorus, 'The One I'm Looking For' for Elsie and Jack, 'Week End' for the chorus, and 'Chirp Chirp,' the best received, for the chirpy Randolph:

Chirp chirp, get together/It's the weather meant for love/Chirp, chirp, get right in it/Say the linnet and the dove./It's the mating season./You'll be held for treason/If you don't capture lovers' rapture.

Swing-conscious Britons will remember the marvellous Benny Goodman recording of perhaps the Ira Gershwin-Charig song best known in Britain, 'Sunny Disposish', which was written for an American revue called *Americana* and interpolated in later British shows. This afforded Ira another opportunity to show off: 'I used [clipping syllables] in "S'Wonderful" and "Sunny Disposish". A few years later I came across some light verse by England's Captain Harry Graham to discover that he had specialized in this lopping off device long before me.'

The Americans Leave the Scene

After 1928, George and Ira Gershwin gradually disappeared from the London theatre scene, as did many other Americans. For many reasons this first golden age of the British-American musical was in decline. Many of the key participants made more insular choices. After *Girl Crazy* in 1930, Guy Bolton chose to work in England, writing with Thompson and Grey, Vivian Ellis, and many other collaborators for Buchanan and Randolph, Henson, and other major British stars of the era – as well as Frances Day, an 'unbelievably blonde' American who duly stunned a generation of British males.

After all, there was the Great Depression – and there was also Hollywood, where the Gershwins were quickly on the scene, and in the long run where they stayed. Even before their original score for *Delicious* in 1931 ('Blah blah blah' is one of Ira's jauntiest, songwriting-kiddingest efforts), with book by Bolton, movie musicals had twice featured Gershwin songs in their scores. In a way, the British-American career of the Gershwins was over.

But there are many loose ends: there was their Broadway outing of 1928, *Treasure Island*, their last for Gertrude Lawrence, which co-starred that Piccadilly Indianan, Clifton Webb. But this failed quickly. Ira called the plot, which portrayed Gertie as a single-minded fortune hunter, unsympathetic: 'the treasure hunt took the proceedings to the Caribbean and after a couple of months took us all to Cains Warehouse [where the artefacts of closed shows were stored]. The songs ['Oh, So Nice', 'A Feeling I'm Falling'] and dances, thanks to a brilliant cast . . . were well, even rapturously received. But, some songwriters to the contrary, numbers alone do not make a show.' Of 'I Don't Think I'll Fall in Love Today', he added a note of pedigree: 'I doubt that the title of this duet would have come to me if at some time or other I hadn't read Chesterton's "A Ballade of Suicide" with its refrain of "I think I will not hang myself today"'.

In 1932, the Gershwins' last New York show for Aarons and Freedley, which also proved to be the last show Aarons and Freedley did together, was *Pardon My English*, a stinker so fragrant that Jack Buchanan left it in Boston. The aptly-titled 'Isn't It a Pity' was its best song. Yet perhaps Ira's words regarding *Treasure Island* were again applicable, for when the Secaucus-rescued score was finally performed in the States a critic called it 'one of their most ingenious scores' in which 'rich choral passages, contrapuntal waltzes, and other complex musical-lyrical passages' made 'a musical stepping stone toward *Porgy and Bess*'.

Neither of these shows has received British attention, nor to any great degree has

their trilogy of satirical operettas, *Strike Up the Band*, *Of Thee I Sing*, and *Let 'Em Eat Cake*. The theatrical history of these shows is strictly Broadway, but a separate study could highlight the freeing of Ira and George's Savoyardism. Only *Of Thee I Sing* made any stir in the States in its own time. (Some stir, a Pulitzer Prize.)

The Gershwins' greatest debt to Gilbert and Sullivan (including soloist-and-choral responses à la *Pinafore*) was probably the 1927 score for *Strike Up The Band*, which closed out of town and materially differed from the moderately successful Broadway reworking of 1930. It is available in an 'authentic' recording made in 1990, directed by John Mauceri (Roxbury Recordings, Elektra Nonesuch, 7559-79273-2).

How British Can You Get?

Perhaps Britain has found these homages too American? There was a performance of the *Let 'Em Eat Cake* overture in 1989, conducted by Michael Tilson Thomas at the Barbican, praised for its 'chromatic language, lively interaction of ideas', and 'spontaneous dramatic combustion. No wonder it proved a bit much for its original audience.' There's little doubt that Glyndebourne's production of *Porgy and Bess* was superb, and that in line with its reverence for George's 'serious' side, Britain has become the world's best advocate for George, Ira, and DuBose Heyward's work as opera. Opera it is, then, outside the scope of this study.

So, truly, is *Rhapsody in Blue*, except that British enthusiasm for that number kept hauling it onto the light musical stage anyhow. It appeared in *Black Birds of 1934*, sung by the Black Birds choir. Beverley Nichols recounts the manner in which Frances Day tracked him across the Channel, insisting that he write special words to the *Rhapsody* so she could sing them. In 1937 he did, and she did, in *Floodlight*.

Still, it seems most fitting and most fun to conclude by considering as musical theatre the last film the Gershwins completed during George's lifetime, the *Damsel in Distress* of 1937. During his several lucrative weeks' work on the script, even Wodehouse came to be pleased at how closely it approximated the country-house-and-snappy-patter of his novel. It was almost inevitably a Wodehouse libretto.

Ira was in his Anglophile element. About 'Nice Work if You Can Get It' he wrote:

Somewhere, I read an illustrated article about a number of cartoons rejected by the humorous weeklies – cartoons and drawings not for the family trade. One submitted to *Punch*, I think, was by George Belcher, whose crayon specialized in delineating London's lowly. In it, two charwomen are discussing the daughter of a third, and the first says she's heard that the discussee 'as become an 'ore.' Whereat the second observes it's nice work if you can get it.

The 'Stiff Upper Lip' funhouse sequence evokes the British-American musical tradition at its best. Fred and Adele Astaire had often been directed on Broadway by Britons. In the American *The Love Letter* of 1921, Teddy Royce (scion of a Gaiety family) gave them their signature dance, the Oompah Trot. An Astaire biographer wrote: 'The Astaires positioned their arms as though they were gripping a bicycle's handlebars and trotted side by side in large circles around the stage to a continuous Germanic oompah oompah beat. It was simple . . . but their lightness of touch guaranteed the success of this innocent exit-sequence.'

The Astaires oompahed year after year, show after show, often with co-stars. In *A Damsel in Distress*, Gracie Allen played Adele's part with style and humour. The idiom of the lyrics for 'Stiff Upper Lip' ('Stout fella! Carry on, old fluff!') is thoroughly patterned upon Bertie Wooster. Ira added: 'Whether the English actually greeted each other or not with old bean or old fluff or old tin of fruit, didn't matter frightfully – we had been conditioned by vaudevillians and comic weeklies to think they did.' Best of all, according to Ira, Wodehouse himself had planned to write

a lyric using his own Woosterisms, but dropped the idea because 'Stiff Upper Lip' was so good.

Perhaps the film's most unusual number is 'The Jolly Tar and the Milkmaid', an out-and-out attempt to mimic an eighteenth-century ballad, based upon meaningless but singable phrases. Ira had plenty of these in hand after looking into D'Urfey's *Pills to Purge Melancholy* (1719-20).

Hey nonny, nonny' was even then on the wane, 'fa la la', whose popularity continued at least to Gilbert and Sullivan, was a hot number. So were hey ding hoe ding, derry derry ding, fadariddle la . . . fa la la lankiy downdilly . . . hey troly loly lo . . . with a humblebum brumblebledum hey . . . huggle duggle ha ha ha.

The easily assimilable nonsense phrase appealed to Ira, as 'It Ain't Necessarily So' had recently proved.

Damsel retains great charm and wondrous specialty numbers, even though a close scrutiny reveals wonders like a procession of left-hand-drive taxis on a studio-bound 'London' street. It also displays the Hollywood British colony of the later 1930s rather well. Ray Noble (a great talent usually wasted in the States, but here more subtle than his silly-ass stereotype), Reginald Gardiner (a transatlantic peripatetic, here allowed a few minutes of inspired lunacy as a closet musical conductor), and Constance Collier (no glamour, but a lot of Margaret Dumont) clash and mesh pleasantly with Fred Astaire, George Burns, and Gracie Allen. And the much-maligned Joan Fontaine does not undermine the movie's high spirits, proving indeed a perfectly acceptable Wodehouse ingenue, sweet and well-meaning. A co-star would have upset the balance.

Damsel in Distress was in fact a fond latter-day enshrining of the classic British-American stage musical of the 'twenties, with nearly all the classic players on board. Striking not a single blue note, it was a light-hearted coda to George and Ira Gershwin's British-American careers.

Jonathan Bignell

Trevor Griffiths's Political Theatre: from 'Oi for England' to 'The Gulf between Us'

This paper examines two plays by Trevor Griffiths, ten years apart in the writing, which responded in different ways to burning contemporary issues. The first, *Oi for England*, though originally seen on television in 1982, was conceived as a theatre text, and was eventually toured to audiences closer to the age (and perhaps to some of the beliefs) of its racist rock-band central characters. *The Gulf between Us*, written in the aftermath of the Gulf War, was staged in Leeds in 1992 as a local theatrical 'event' at the West Yorkshire Playhouse, under Griffiths's own direction. Jonathan Bignell looks at the ways in which the different nature of these occasions and audiences, and the different ways in which the plays can be viewed as 'political theatre' – in particular, the new demands made by *The Gulf* upon critics who arrived with a type-cast view of its author – in both cases militated against a successful political statement being conveyed. Jonathan Bignell completed a PhD on narrative in film and television fictions in 1989, and since then has lectured in English and Media Studies in the English Department of the University of Reading. His research interests are in literary theory, and film and television analysis.

TEN YEARS separated Trevor Griffiths's *Oi for England* and his return to original stage work with *The Gulf between Us* in 1992.[1] A comparison between these two plays shows the spectrum of his political involvement with the theatrical medium, in terms of subject, form, and the audience groups which were targeted in each case. I shall demonstrate the similarities in intention and formal structure of the plays, and discuss the implications for Griffiths's particular theatre practice of the different performance contexts and audience groups which the two productions involved.

Both *Oi for England* and *The Gulf between Us* dealt with political situations that were contemporary, and were written as a result of Griffiths's sense that a response from the left was urgent. He said of *The Gulf*, 'It was an enjoined play, a play that I had to write for my reasons. . . . The way you write depends on what is urgent'.[2] Ten years before, in 1982, after attending a conference on 'Race in the Classroom', he had written *Oi* , saying

After a long involvement with nuanced scripts like *Country* and *The Cherry Orchard*, not to mention the *Reds* saga, I felt the need to write something more urgent and immediate, and there's nothing more urgent than racism.[3]

This sense of urgency not only demonstrates that Griffiths felt a personal involvement with his subject. The political subjects of the two plays were different, though I shall demonstrate structural links between them below. But they both arose from a sense of political responsibility, to which the 'urgency' testifies. Responsibility entails the notion of response, and in both plays Griffiths sought to engage the audience in a process of responding to political subjects in new ways. Both plays involved constructing a particular range of discourses which competed to define their political subject. This process of construction for the creation of audience engagement is the aspect of political theatre on which I shall concentrate.

Both plays were explicitly taking issue with the representation of political issues, racist violence in one case and the Gulf War in the other, and this is signalled by the fact that they both were first performed one year after the events they portrayed. The anniversary implicitly linked the plays to a historical process in which an event was already set into historical time, and spoken about in particular ways. Griffiths's works sought to explore and debate existing and recognizable representations of racist youth culture in *Oi for England*, and representations of the Gulf War in *The Gulf between Us*.

The Drama of Political Engagement

Oi had been screened on ITV before it became a theatrical event, while *The Gulf* marked a return to theatre as the primary medium. During the 1970s Griffiths had used TV drama as his preferred medium because of its much larger and more diverse audience. Theatre had seemed 'incapable, as a social institution, of reaching, let alone *mobilizing*, large popular audiences'.[4]

The use of TV meant that Griffiths chose naturalistic forms for his plays at that time, since this was the form with which the TV audience was most familiar, and provided a recognizable environment into which characters could be placed. But character was used as a vehicle for exploring ideas and not (as often seemed the case in TV fiction) for its own sake, or for the sake of involving the audience in a story. In this sense Griffiths's work returned to the original radical purposes of the naturalistic form, in exploring the contradictions of contemporary social issues in a way which might now be termed realist rather than through the comfortable naturalism of contemporary TV fiction.

During the 1980s, TV drama became more formally innovative, through such plays as Dennis Potter's *Singing Detective* or Alan Bleasdale's recent *GBH*. As a result, perhaps, in the late 1980s and early 1990s Griffiths was unsuccessful in getting his work screened on television. His 1985 play about the Miners' Strike for the BBC was never made – though its title, *The Truth and Other Fictions*, became the subtitle of *The Gulf*. He was therefore driven back to

theatre as the medium for his work, and to the different audience and institutional constraints which this entailed. Not least of these constraints is the importance of the authorial and directorial signature in gaining funding and audiences. Griffiths not only both wrote and directed *The Gulf*, but to do so returned to Leeds where he had previously worked.

Oi had been conceived as a theatre text before becoming a TV play, and this was for very particular reasons. Griffiths had intended the play to be performed for schools, as a response to recruitment campaigns by right-wing organizations looking for youth support. The play was toured around youth clubs and community centres, gradually being changed in the process, each performance being followed by a discussion on the issues it was intended to raise.

This was explained in part by Griffiths's interest in the developmental aspects of theatre in education, where performance is often preceded by classroom work, and follow-up work is designed to extend thinking to which the performance gives a form. But the discussions are also evidence of Griffiths's intention that theatre should not simply present ideas and come to conclusions, but engage the audience in a process of thought and debate which can lead to action. However, without the careful preparation and structured continuing teaching which enfolds TIE productions, the audiences of young people who saw *Oi* were not only confused about what the play was engaging with in their experience, but also lacked the specific skills to understand theatrical representation.

There's no sense at all that we are watching a piece of theatre. It's assumed that the actors are real-life skinheads. There's also a constant banter going on in the background as the actors struggle to hold the attention of an audience that clearly doesn't know quite how to react to what's happening on stage.[5]

The very notion of representation itself was unfamiliar to this audience in the context of live performance. Therefore, the play was unsuccessful as a political intervention, since it did not provoke debate about issues in the lives of the audience:

Those who spoke had to be pressed into connecting [the play] with issues like unemployment or racism and were much happier talking about how it confirmed their own experience of skinheads as 'nutters' full stop.[6]

Oi was also unsuccessful as theatre, since its naturalistic theatrical form could not easily be decoded, and the cabaret style which gradually replaced naturalism during the tour moved the play towards musical performance interspersed with dialogue.

The Gulf also featured a discussion at one of its performances, on the subject of press coverage of the Gulf War.[7] However, in this case the discussion preceded the play, and was billed as a separate event. It did not use the play as a structure which provided representations for the audience to adduce and debate, but instead encouraged them to stay for the matinee performance which then became a proof or disproof of points made by the discussion's speakers.

There was only one discussion, which seemed to be attended by particular groups who already held a sophisticated opinion about its topic. The discussion was arranged by the Yorkshire and Humberside Campaign for Press Freedom, and a number of journalists attended. The speakers on the platform were professional journalists and academics, some with well-known names and reputations (like Tariq Ali and the poet Tony Harrison). The event was therefore appropriate to the large and successful venue of the West Yorkshire Playhouse, and we can perhaps justly claim that it reinforced the views of an audience likely to attend a Griffiths play. If this is the case, it was an event at the opposite end of the spectrum from the discussions of *Oi*, and, for very different reasons, equally unsuccessful at mobilizing an audience group not already targeted by political theatre.

Both *Oi* and *The Gulf* featured cultural groups alien to the mainstream audience. With the exception of a young black woman in a minor role, *Oi* showed young skinheads involved in the riots of the summer of 1981,

and a right-wing organizer of musical events and political violence. The four main characters were members of an Oi-rock band rehearsing their songs in a dank cellar which was the only set. Their style of dress, language, and outlook were aggressive and signalled racism and violence. Their music was loud and rough, with provocative and aggressive lyrics.

Theatre Forms in 'Oi' and 'The Gulf'

The use of a particular critical naturalistic form allowed Griffiths to show how and why disaffected young people might create and gain self-identification from a violent and racist subculture, and the spatial containment of the traditional room setting suggested the claustrophobia and poverty of their environment. Thus, the play coherently represented this alien subculture through naturalism, and also demonstrated the contradictions which membership of it entailed by focusing on a skinhead character, Finn, whose background and psychology were partly at odds with such membership.

Finn came from an Irish family, and the uneasy relationship of Irishness to Britishness enabled Griffiths to use his characterization to challenge the simple nationalism of skinhead culture. Finn gave the audience access to the alien skinhead culture through sympathy and identification with his difficult position. The Irishness which enabled his distance from skinhead culture was mainly expressed by the psychologizing which belongs to the naturalistic form.

The Gulf also represented cultural otherness. The play was set in an unnamed Arab country (probably Iraq), so that its British characters were destabilized and defamiliarized in the course of the action by their contact with Arab characters – who were initially 'other', but progressively presented as at least equally available to audience identification.

At the moral centre of [the play] are Arabs, who are experiencing this crushing, horrific, punitive, exemplary war which is being handed down to them by the Western Alliance for reasons and values that really don't stand up to even the most cursory scrutiny.[8]

Two builders, stranded in the country by the beginning of the Gulf War, have been offered exit visas by the Arab administration in exchange for quickly repairing a bombed Shia shrine. The shrine had been a bomb-shelter, but also a covert weapons store. The manipulation of information by both East and West is a central theme of the play, which exposes the prejudices of both sides. The main character, holding together the contradictory claims of the two sides, is the intinerant gilder O'Toole, who doubles as The Gukha, a narrating storytelling figure from Arabic literature who lived forever, and points out similarities between the Gulf War and the Crusades.

This was the only representative of non-western representational forms in the play, for Griffiths did not use cross-cultural signifying forms of theatre but chose to emphasize instead the disjuncture between western and eastern political discourses, and their similar use of disinformation and media manipulation. Since each rhetorical construction was shown to be unable justly to account for the conflict, the Gukha character became potentially a vehicle for a meta-narrative about the naturalistic action, where the action could be contextualized and historicized in an alien, non-naturalistic mode.

Resolutions as Irresolution

But he did not take this role, since in terms of his character-identity he was both physically and mentally unable to perform such a structural function: his eyesight and memory were impaired. Just as the Finn character in *Oi* could not resolve his contradictory identifications, there was a physical splitting and doubling of the western O'Toole and the Arab Gukha in *The Gulf*. Additionally, at the level of structure, the Gukha in *The Gulf* was unable to represent a structural resolution of the alternative histories and discourses which the play contained, though the play's theatrical form seemed to enable this.

The endings of the two plays show a similar use of negation and irresolution, which demonstrates in formal terms the same yoked contradictions seen above in terms of character. *Oi* ended with Finn alone on the set, playing a tape of Irish folk music as he tidies up: but the music seemed to prompt him to destroy the band's equipment in a frenzy of aggression. 'When he turns on the tape it's his frustration at having to deny that more tender, lyrical side of himself that, as much as anything, provokes his violent outburst'.[9] By destroying the instruments he makes his band unviable as a way out of his environment, clinching a decision which has already been prepared by his refusal to let the band play at a gig organized by a racist political grouping. No theatrical sign, either in dialogue, gesture, or music, suggested that an alternative or hopeful future awaited him.

Similarly, *The Gulf* ended with an Arab woman doctor pulling the burnt remains of a child from the bombed shrine, and then delivering an impassioned tirade against western aggression. It had already been made clear however that the use of the shrine as shelter and arms-dump was a cynical manouevre to allow precisely this emotive appeal, and the local population of the country were being duped by the rhetoric of their leaders in the same way that the working-class builders from Britain were deluded by *The Sun*'s jingoistic racism.

The ending of *Oi* counterposed violent Oi-rock against pastoral Irish folk, with Finn caught between them and enacting an anarchistic, negative response. The ending of *The Gulf* counterposed the pathos and emotion of the dead child with the long polemical address to the audience by Dr. Aziz, shifting the audience from one regime of spectatorship to another, from emotional involvement to political argument, and refusing a pathos which might anneal and resolve the play's contrasts.

These comparisons of characterization and structure show that Griffiths's move from TV to theatre, and from critical naturalism to a mixed form, entailed a continuity of political intent and audience positioning. Neither play offered straight-forward identification with a main charac-ter, or a conclusive resolution to the action. However, the purpose of this, to enable political debate beyond the performance, was apparently vitiated by the venues and audience groups of the two different pro-ductions. To take this problem further, we need next to examine the institutional con-texts and reception of the two plays.

Institutions and Reception

The funding for the tour of *Oi* came partly from local government, but controversy arose over two issues. Councillors objected to the play's strong language, which they found distasteful. More significantly, they did not believe that the piece opposed racism, seeming instead simply to present it. Their objections revolved around whether a young black audience would understand the play as anti-racist, and whether the audience would take part in the post-performance discussions.

They would go to the play for the music and wouldn't stay for the discussion. It would go over their heads anyway. They wouldn't under-stand the argument. Anyway, why the hell should you have to explain it afterwards?[10]

Unfortunately, as we have seen, this criti-cism seemed justified by audience reaction to some of the performances.

Local newspapers attempted to generate a similar controversy over *The Gulf*, accusing the council of spending money on a venue which offered a play that insulted the war dead. When asked for comment, the deputy Conservative leader of Leeds City Council replied:

It's difficult to comment having not seen the play but it does seem insensitive for this sort of pro-duction to be put out on the public purse at this time. This is like stabbing our heroes in the back.[11]

There was a small demonstration outside the theatre when the play began its run.

However, in the context of the West York-shire Playhouse, very different from the venues and audiences for the tour of *Oi*, the audiences were consistently large and accepted the play's contents.

Professional critics identified problems with the structure and relative strengths of performers in *The Gulf*. The soundscape of explosions and air raids provided an atmo-sphere of tension and danger, reinforced by projected images of air attacks, and signified the overwhelming aggression that the characters on stage had to find a language to explain or justify. But the Arab characters intended to be at the centre of the thematic structure were seen as underwritten textu-ally and thus weak in performance.

Critics were also confused by the mixed theatrical modes, since naturalistic action co-existed with the 'magic realism' of the trans-historical Gukha figure, and the piece could also be seen as a 'work play', with the builders constructing a wall on stage in the real time of the performance. The shifting emotional and polemical registers seemed disjointed.

The play's reviewers tried to identify its message, since the subject implied that it would draw coherent conclusions about the Gulf War. They failed to find a message except for a condemnation of the self-serving adventurism of both sides, and this was felt to be inadequate. Trevor Griffiths's name and reputation is central to the pattern of their reactions, as I shall discuss below.

Reviews of the TV version of *Oi* con-centrated on the power to shock which a coherent and naturalistic piece about skin-heads could achieve. While the play was seen to give access to a world alien to the reviewers and the play's majority audience, the effect was described as repellent and not as enabling thought. The reviewer for *The Times* wrote:

Oi for England . . . is an appalling play. I don't mean only the foul language, which is grinding and unnecessary. It is appalling because it makes explicit what other plays about the fuelling of anarchy in Britain have been content to leave implicit. . . . The intensity of the hatred it encapsulates left me feeling utterly dismayed.[12]

There are some structural parallels with *The Gulf* here. *Oi* showed a group who were distant and alarming to the viewer, but a group who aggressively espoused nationalistic values ('England for the English', etc.). The Irish background of the main character gave him the ambiguous relationship to this identity which allowed him to reject it, though he had no alternative identity to espouse. *The Gulf* showed Britons who were alien to their environment, and an environment alien to the audience. The conjunction of O'Toole and The Gukha was a pairing of an outsider, an intinerant Irishman, with a non-human immortal narrator from an alien literary tradition. This pairing suggested that different nationalities, cultures, and time-frames would be resolved, perhaps by the linkage of story-telling to history-writing which the commenting Gukha enabled.

In practice, however, the structure of the play was disrupted and left open by the failure of The Gukha to offer a meta-language with a clear political meaning which could account for the diverse registers of the play, a disruption which Griffiths called 'anarchism (not anarchy). I feel that impulse is celebrated within the figure of The Gukha'.[13] But, as Benedict Nightingale commented in *The Times*: 'the piece is more weakened than enriched by Griffiths's attempts to push the proceedings in odd, unrealistic directions'.[14] What Griffiths called the 'anarchism' of The Gukha, like the anarchic destruction enacted by Finn, could not, by definition, produce a closure for the audience.

Anarchic action had this effect in *Oi*, and anarchic character and form had the same effect in *The Gulf*. In both cases a political message was not presented, precisely because Griffiths intended the audience to leave the theatre still troubled, trying to connect the play's action to their own lives. But the youthful audience of *Oi* were unable to do this, and the more competent audience of *The Gulf* seem to have viewed irresolution as an effect of bad writing or direction.

The term 'political theatre' can be used to denote three different ideas. Its first meaning would suggest a performance which deals thematically with ideas recognized as political by the audience. Here, the audience's ideological framework is a condition of recognizing themes as political rather than simply realistic. Political theatre in this sense must represent a comprehensible world and make it available for political debate in the play. Both *The Gulf* and *Oi* represent a world which the characters perceive from political points of view. Griffiths's form of critical naturalism is designed to represent a coherent world, but, unlike mainstream TV fictional naturalism, this form allows characters to be shown working through their reality from political positions.

The second sense of 'political' describes an active relationship between the performance and the audience. This kind of political theatre would be a performance which produces political effects in and for the lives of the audience. Both *The Gulf* and *Oi* were intended to engage and change the audience in this sense. The discussions after the touring performances of *Oi* clearly demonstrate Griffiths's desire to engage audiences in this way, and remnants of the same desire can be seen in the discussion and the programme notes of *The Gulf*.

In order for such a stage-audience relationship to be constructed, the audience needs to be able to decode the play's theatrical form, and relate its concerns to their own experience and thoughts. It is here that levels of competence are important, and the touring performances of *Oi* had problems in creating an effective relationship with an audience lacking in competence. Without it, they failed even to recognize that the play was dealing with political issues (political theatre in the first sense).

Thirdly, political theatre can denote a performance in which theatricality – the fact of representing in the medium of theatre – is foregrounded. The audience here are thus engaged in a self-conscious process of questioning their own modes of understanding theatrical representation, and questioning their assumptions about what theatre as a medium might be. A high level of competence is required for this kind of political theatre, and works which undertake to explore it are often those most valued by academics and intellectuals – and least valued by the majority in western culture. *Oi* did not start out as political theatre in this third sense, though the need to achieve an effective stage-audience relationship on the tour led to some urgent thinking about the politics of the theatrical form which had been employed.

Issues of Empowerment and Expectation

I would like to conclude by exploring the ways in which *The Gulf* moved between the different senses of political theatre, which show how Griffiths has been constrained by his own distinguished reputation as a maker of political theatre.

Griffiths felt in 1992 that one of the so-called achievements of the continuing Conservative administration had been to disenable people from seeing their lives in a political way. Even the discourse of politicians had become ruled by economic and administrative pragmatism: politics was not any longer to do with finding the most just way of living and organizing society, but 'is now the politics of the pocket-book – there is no broader morality. This is the achievement of Thatcherism'.[15]

It was of course clearly political to pronounce the slogans of the 1980s, like 'There is no alternative' or 'There is no such thing as society, there are only individuals and families'. But Griffiths felt that these redefinitions of the British scene were now so generally accepted as to make an oppositional political discourse seem pointless or irrelevant.

A serious job of disempowerment has gone on, not just culturally but politically and socially. . . . It has left us with our political culture in tatters. We're in a sort of wasteland where people have got to start recreating the world.[16]

Political theatre in the first sense, of seeing the world from different political points of view, would thus fail to represent the reality accepted by a majority. The critical naturalism of *The Truth and Other Fictions*, Griffiths's TV play on the Miners' Strike, would seem inappropriate. The play was never produced, and Griffiths's inability to get work on television also prevented him from engaging its audience in political thought – in political theatre in the second sense.

His return to the theatre with *The Gulf* exploits the fact that the medium has always been more open to experiment and political intervention: 'In the absence of being able to get a foot in the door of TV, maybe theatre is the remaining site of struggle.'[17] But the diminishing funds and audiences for oppositional work forced him, perhaps unknowingly, to exploit the fact that theatre is also bourgeois and traditionalist, in its focus on big-name authors and well-made plays. Coming as did the final version of *The Gulf* from a well-known practitioner with associations with Leeds, it would have been surprising for the West Yorkshire Playhouse to have refused it.

The play could thus be seen as political theatre in all three senses distinguished above: it presented a world from political points of view, it sought to engage the audience in debate, and (unusually for Griffiths) it also mixes, contrasts and reflects upon its own theatrical form, most obviously through the figure of The Gukha. 'It's a web of specific things meshed with something more abstract. I think it's the nearest I've got to magic realism.'[18]

The competences of *The Gulf*'s audiences were apparently sufficient to read the play as political theatre in the first two senses. But some reviewers presented the unusual form of the play as a failure, because their expectation was that Griffiths would provide a rational and involving statement about the politics of the Gulf War in accordance with his past success at political theatre in the first two senses.

Such a statement did not arrive. The understanding of Griffiths's signature, the fact that the play was 'signed' with his name as author and director, allowed the critics to close down the meanings of the production. Its anarchic form and mixed registers were not perceived as political theatre in the third sense, but as Griffiths's failure to live up to the meanings of his own signature. Because the reviewers perceived the name 'Trevor Griffiths' to entail political theatre only in the first two senses, the possibility of the third, successfully achieved or not, seemed not to occur to them.

Noting the repressive control of radical theatre practice by showing that it is recuperated as the eccentric individual voice of an author or director is a commonplace theoretical insight. But it is significant to note the problems of *Oi* on tour in contrast to *The Gulf*, as two opposite ends of a spectrum of Griffiths's political theatre. The young audiences' lack of competence in decoding *Oi* on tour demonstrates one limit to Griffiths's critical naturalism: it can only work with an audience able to read it as such. The reaction of a specialist audience represented by some of the reviewers of *The Gulf* demonstrates the limit at the other end of the spectrum: their knowledge of Griffiths's authorship seemed to prevent them from bringing their highly-developed competences to bear on a new work in which he attempted to grapple with the usual first two meanings of political theatre by integrating them with a third sense.

Notes and References

1. *Oi for England* was screened on ITV on 17 April 1982, and its first theatrical tour ran from 12 May to 5 June 1982. *The Gulf between Us* ran from 16 January to 8 February 1992 at the West Yorkshire Playhouse.

2. Trevor Griffiths, quoted in Sarah Hemming, 'Caught in the Crossfire', *The Independent*, 8 January 1992.

3. Griffiths, quoted in 'Mistaken Identities', *City Limits*, 16-22 April 1982.

4. Griffiths, Preface to *Through the Night and Such Impossibilities* (Faber, 1977), p. 7.

5. M. Poole 'Trying to Get under their Skins', *The Guardian*, 7 June 1982.

6. Ibid.

7. The discussion took place on Saturday 25 January 1992.

8. Griffiths, programme note for *The Gulf between Us*.

9. Griffiths, 'Mistaken Identities', op. cit.

10. Cllr. Jack Brown, quoted in '*Oi* Hits a Cultural Brick Wall', *The Guardian*, 8 October 1982.

11. Cllr. Keith Louden, quoted in 'Gulf Play "Stabs Heroes in Back"', *Yorkshire Evening Post*, 10 January 1992.

12. *The Times*, 17 April 1982.

13. Griffiths, 'Caught in the Crossfire', op. cit.

14. Benedict Nightingale, 'Misdirected in the Desert', *The Times*, 23 January 1992.

15. Griffiths, 'Caught in the Crossfire', op. cit.

16. Griffiths, quoted in 'New World Order', *Northern Star*, 9-16 January 1992.

17. Ibid.

18. Ibid.

Martin Rohmer

Wole Soyinka's 'Death and the King's Horseman', Royal Exchange Theatre, Manchester

In large part due to the relative lack of productions in Europe, the plays of Wole Soyinka have mostly been approached from a literary point of view rather than analyzed as theatrical events. Because the plays rely heavily on non-verbal conventions, this neglect of visual and acoustic patterns promotes an incomplete understanding of Soyinka's idea of theatre. Here, for the first time, a play by Soyinka is analyzed from the point of view of performance – specifically, the production of *Death and the King's Horseman* staged at the Royal Exchange Theatre, Manchester, in 1990. Martin Rohmer examines the transformation of playscript into *mise-en-scène*, focusing in particular on the use of music and dance, but looking also at the production as an intercultural event – asking not only how far a European company has to rely on African performing skills, but how far a European cast and audience is capable of a proper understanding of the play. This article is a revised version of a lecture delivered at the Conference of the Association for the Study of the New Literatures in English, held in Bayreuth in June 1992. Martin Rohmer studied Drama, German Literature, Anthropology, and Philosophy in Munich, and Theatre, Film and TV Studies at the University of Glasgow, before completing his MA in Munich in 1992. Presently he is a Research Assistant at the University of Bayreuth, where he is working on a PhD on the performing arts in Zimbabwe.

ON 22 NOVEMBER 1990, the Royal Exchange Theatre (RET) in Manchester was the scene for the second British production of Wole Soyinka's *Death and the King's Horseman*. Although written in 1973, the play had only once before been staged in Britain, in a production by Chris Kamlongera in July 1983 for the Drama Department of the University of Hull. And so far as the press were concerned, the RET production, directed by Phyllida Lloyd, was generally regarded as the British premiere.

For western directors the staging of the play causes problems on a formal as well as thematic level, the main obstacle being the dramaturgical importance of music and dance as the two other basic means, apart from verbal dialogue, of communication in African culture. These three elements in fact constitute the fundamental pattern of communication throughout the play, and its success or failure in production will mainly depend on how the interrelation of each of these stylistic devices to one another is established.

The basic question is thus to what extent the unfolding of the tragic action leads to a shift within the different levels of expression – or, to put it another way, in what ways does a change within the patterns of communication reflect the development of the characters? This paper tries to outline this interrelation, the way it was realized on one of Britain's leading stages and the dramaturgical implications for the cast and the audience.

By her own admission, Phyllida Lloyd had little experience with African theatre in general or Yoruba culture in particular: but she was encouraged by Peter Badejo, who agreed to participate by acting as Nigerian cultural advisor as well as playing the Praise-Singer. He was in charge of the choreography, while Muraina Oyelami was 'Musical Director and Composer'. One could call this an extended *mise-en-scène*.

A major factor in determining Phyllida Lloyd's decision to direct *Death and the King's Horseman* was the very architecture of the Royal Exchange Theatre:

This is obviously a very particular theatre space, a particular design. I've been directing a lot of classical plays in the last couple of years, and I was looking for a modern play that had something important to say and also did it in a way that would do justice to the physical life here. And the fact that part of this play is set in a market place, and this theatre is built in a nineteenth-century market just seemed somehow too good to be true.

The Meaning of Space

The significance of the space in which a performance takes place and the fact that it plays an important role in the conveyance of meaning is generally accepted. Yet as Lloyd has pointed out, it is of special interest for her production. Moreover it is widely known that Soyinka, not only as the author but as an experienced theatre practitioner, has clear ideas about spatial issues in the staging of his plays, as I will discuss below. The architectural peculiarity of the RET is as a 'building within a building' – for the theatre is constructed inside the huge Victorian hall that was once the city's famous and busy Cotton Exchange. To avoid the colossal echo-effect the stage has a separate acoustic entity.

An examination of the Victorian building reveals its function as a conveyor of meaning on various levels: on the level of urban development, with its central situation close to the market and in the heart of the inner city, accessible from St. Ann's Square and Cross Street; on the optical level, with its visual appearance emblematic of strength and prosperity; and on the historical level, thanks to its age, the tradition of the Cotton Exchange being as a busy market and distribution centre for goods from the colonies, at a time when Manchester was one of the wealthiest communities in Britain or even the old Empire. As Phyllida Lloyd points out, this historical aspect made the RET an ironically apt venue for the play.

A main RET strategy is, however, to attract people by using the huge foyer for non-theatrical events. Through architectural and programmatic channels the RET tries to create an 'everyday space'[1] by organizing exhibitions, concerts, lectures, children's shows, etc., and through the craft centre in the foyer. According to its own estimate[2] of 15,000 people passing through the foyer each week, one has to admit that the RET's purpose of maintaining its function as a magnet for the citizens has been fully successful: there is hardly a local person who is not familiar with the place's interior.

The modern glass building that forms the inner theatre space is constructed as a theatre in the round, and this corresponds to Soyinka's intentions for his play. A director with experience of both picture frame and arena staging, Soyinka leaves no doubt about his preference: 'As a decidedly anti-proscenium stage artist, I hope to see fewer and fewer of those mind-constructors left in the world.'[3]

Concerning *Death and the King's Horseman*, the communicative advantages of the arena stage match both the metaphysical concept of what Soyinka defines as 'ritual drama', and more particularly the notion of what he terms the audience's choric function:

The so-called audience is itself an integral part of that arena of conflict; it contributes spiritual strength to the protagonist through its choric reality which must first be conjured up and established, defining and investing the arena through offerings and incantations.[4]

In Soyinka's plays with metaphysical implications (as opposed to his satiric comedies), the arena's function as a magic microcosm cannot be overestimated. During the performance it is turned into a spiritually energetic space where the actors may re-enact the basic conflicts of Yoruba mythology to regain cosmic harmony and to bridge the gap between the gods and man.

The conditions of a theatre in the round and the spatial integration of the foyer avoid the conventional and paralyzing illusionism which is so easily created by the proscenium

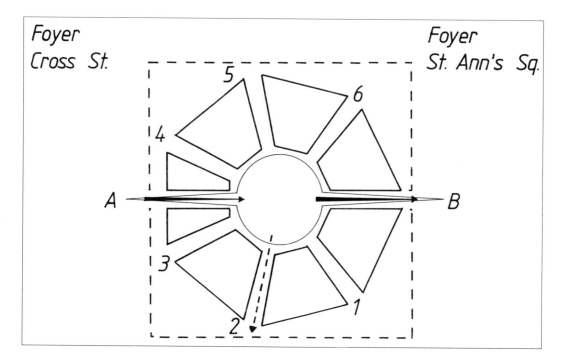

Foyer
Cross St.

Foyer
St. Ann's Sq.

arch form. Another dramaturgical advantage of the arena stage is its flexibility concerning the setting, whereby Soyinka's demand for rapid scene changes[5] can be fully realized.

The spatial conditions of the RET thus perfectly match Soyinka's aesthetic concept in relation to its tradition as an Exchange, or market, with a colonial history which correlates ironically with part of the play's setting; and owing to the building's roots in the city's community, the functioning of its stage as a 'magic microcosm' which positions the protagonist in the centre, surrounded by the choric circle of the audience, and through its huge foyer, which allows a spatial extension of the play's action and so intensifies its dynamics.

A Personal or Communal Tragedy?

Of the five scenes in which Soyinka has constructed his play, the first, third, and fifth take place in a 'Yoruba setting', while the second and fourth are a reflection of the isolated life of Europeans in Nigeria. The play starts with a celebration on the market place: Elesin, the protagonist and chief horseman of the king – one of the highest positions in the community – enters with his drummers and praise-singers, and soon the place is filled with market women and others who join in the festive atmosphere. It is only after a while that the audience begin to suspect the reason behind these celebrations – which becomes completely clear in the second scene, when Simon Pilkings, the District Officer in his bungalow, urges his native Sergeant Amusa and his house-boy Joseph to tell him the true meaning of the unusual drum rhythms which are audible, and which gradually start worrying him.

Their response finally makes not only Pilkings but the audience aware that this merry atmosphere is nothing less than a preparation for death – since, according to custom, the horseman has to follow the king, who has died shortly before, by committing ritual suicide. The play tells the story of a failure – Elesin's failure to fulfil the demands of this ritual, due to a combination of external and personal factors.

In the RET production the Yoruba scenes were symbolized by a yellow circle (the intention, however, was 'earth colour') of stage size, marked on the floor, with two arrows leading through opposite doors (see illustration above). The basic idea behind this was, according to the director, the interpretation of the action as Elesin's spiritual journey, which should have led him through the door (A) to the centre point, where he is supposed to die. The correct path of his spirit to the ancestors would have been straight through door (B), but the Horseman is distracted, diverted by following his egoistic motives: seeing a beautiful young girl among the market women, he proposes to marry her before his death, and as it is his last day on earth the market women – although annoyed by this behaviour – don't dare deny him this last request.

However, Iyaloja, the leader of the market women, warns him not to cling to life and so unbalance the communal welfare by not following the ritual – a classical dramaturgic convention of Soyinka's, preparing the audience to expect what is being warned against. The importance of Elesin's egoism, clearly visualized in Manchester, gave a theatrical hint of this outcome: the bridal chamber was in the wrong direction. As Phyllida Lloyd commented: 'It's like a kind of pit-stop and possibly one of the contributory factors of his downfall.'

The production starts with an entry dance of Elesin and his friends through the foyer and around the theatre – some of the spectators joining in, and extending the dance to a procession, while others have already taken their seats inside. Indeed Elesin enters the stage after one circulation through door (A), while the first scene takes place in the centre.

By the end of Scene i, lengths of indigo cloth for the wedding have been rolled out from the side, visualizing Elesin's diversion. And no action could make Elesin's failure clearer than his re-entry in the fourth scene, when he is brutally pushed through door (B) by Simon Pilkings, who has arrested the horseman to prevent him from carrying out what he considers a barbaric custom. But this time Elesin is pushed in the opposite direction – back into the circle, back into the life that he now hates so desperately.

Even more clearly than by means of spatial indicators, Elesin's downfall is represented by a change in his personality.

The crucial shift from the beginning to the end, which is already clear in Soyinka's script, was significantly transmitted in Lloyd's production through the depiction of the tragedy of the protagonist. Elesin's dramatic decline during the action could thus be followed in three steps. In the beginning, when the celebrants enter the arena, Elesin is carried in triumphantly on a friend's shoulders. As the market women are kneeling around him, the effect of his raising is even further intensified. And later we see him standing in his (alari) clothes of honour, arrogantly claiming the bride. In the end it is Elesin himself who is kneeling before Iyaloja, covered with shame. The configuration has been inverted.

A threefold downward trend in the choreography of the chief actor may thus be perceived – a dramatic diminution on a vertical and horizontal level. The first step shows much individual freedom of movement on the horizontal level, with the totality of the foyer's spatial facilities being employed. Carried shoulder-high, Elesin towers above all the others, the highest position that is possible on the vertical level. In the second stage his arrogance is making him stand stiff and static – preparing the ground for his ensuing destruction and humiliation, completed in the final scene when, kneeling, he is unable to move, weighed down by heavy chains – on both the horizontal and vertical level the lowest position possible.

Two stage directions at the beginning of the script illustrate Elesin's personality, the first being the introductory description:

Elesin Oba enters along a passage before the market, pursued by his drummers and praise-singers. He is a man of enormous vitality, speaks, dances, and sings with that infectious enjoyment of life which accompanies all his action. (p. 147)

This stage direction emphasizes the chief actor's expressive versatility, gained through the traditional education which he is likely to have enjoyed, which has taught him to employ the power not only of the word but of music and dance as well to represent himself. The term has to be seen in an African semantic context. While the European might take the word 'vitality' as a a broad state of being, the African associates it with an aesthetic concept.[6]

The versatility and expressive strength of Elesin's body language are stressed in another stage direction, where Soyinka focuses attention on the perfect interaction between the various expressive forms by describing the way the drummer takes over the Horseman's dance steps and integrates them in his own, improvised rhythm: 'He performs like a born raconteur' (p. 149).

Expressing the Community's Wholeness

But it is not only the protagonist himself who is depicted as versatile and vital: the Yoruba community is portrayed as an organic whole. Soyinka thus requires that the market women should sing and dance around Elesin. In West Africa the circle is an important element for any kind of theatrical action – a microcosm, symbolizing harmony, unity, and communal experience:[7]

South of the Sahara, solo-and-circle, or solo-and-line, or solo-and-solo forms of dancing mirror melodic call-and-response. . . . Persons singing the chorus frequently double as the circling group who surround or are led by the master singer.[8]

The patterns of call-and-response and solo-and-circle could be observed quite often in Manchester. Frequently the market women created a choric circle around the chief actor Elesin, either dancing or – as, for instance, in the Not-I bird episode, which is based on oral tradition with Elesin as the story-teller – sitting. The system of call-and-response is not confined to solo-and-circle, but may be employed by two single actors or two groups. In any situation, however, it indicates an undisturbed natural state between the communicants.

In the production the cyclic structure was broken when harmony became threatened. Elesin's claim to the bride, surprising and unforeseen, is an affront to the others. It is significant that, as a consequence of his behaviour, the women gather around Iyaloja,

Top: Elesin carried in triumphantly on a friend's shoulders. Middle: Elesin arrogantly claims his bride in his clothes of honour. Bottom: the shamed Elesin kneeling before Iyaloja. Photos: Jan Woollams.

while the Horseman sees himself in an isolated position: the circle has been changed to
a two-block structure, which does not reflect
a common, harmonious action of one group
but a conflict of two in opposition.

It is thus noteworthy that shortly before
his frank and proud claim Elesin shows his
first signs of indifference and lack of will
to communicate by not responding to the
honours of the women who are dancing
around him. Instead his eyes lustfully follow
the bride dancing around him with the other
market women – a serious neglect of conventions between chief actor and choric
group, a departure from the ideal communicative pattern. Yet these two situations
cannot destroy the basically harmonious
atmosphere among the Yoruba characters:
the irritations are soon reconciled, and the
market women, once having blessed Elesin's
marriage with the bride, commence the
wedding preparations.

The *mise-en-scène* tried to prompt the
audience's awareness of a basically positive
communication among the Yoruba community in the first part of the play by other dramaturgic means. Firstly, expressive forms
were combined and thereby given an
emphatic function. Thus Elesin's words 'my
rein is loosened' were supported by the
chorus's imitations of riders – a highly
stylized movement without any intention of
creating theatrical illusion. In a similar way
the storytelling episodes of the first scene
employed this technique of doubling expressive forms.

Secondly, the relationship between Elesin
as the patron and his drummers[9] is characterized in the play by mutual dependence
and friendship. While the accompaniments
are basically rhythmic, it is the lead-
drummer who speaks with his instrument
(hence the 'talking drum'). In Manchester he
was therefore not confined to his role as a
musician, but participated in the action on
stage as both actor (although he never spoke
a single word) and musician.

Thirdly – and the most obvious structural
embodiment of call-and-response as a
pattern of an harmonic communication –
antiphonal singing was employed at the
beginning of Scene iii, when two groups of
market women came in through opposite
doors.

The Community Paralyzed

In the fifth scene of the play the audience is
confronted with a paralyzed community
and two deaths – those of the protagonist,
who has failed, and his son, who has tried
to retain his family's honour by committing
suicide in his father's place. It should be
noted that Elesin is not merely silenced
(metaphorically and literally), but that all
the modes of expression which were multi-
faceted in the beginning have been reduced
to the one that dominates and creates the
tragic atmosphere – the dirge of the chorus,
which 'rises and falls' as prescribed in
several stage directions in the final act. Not
only has Elesin's power of language been
broken, neither is he able to move: his
expressive versatility has been destroyed.

The question arises, whether Elesin's
destruction influences the Yoruba community and, if so, to what extent it is able to
make good this serious disruption. In a
speech in the fifth scene accusing Elesin of
weakness and of betraying the entire community, Iyaloja reveals the language and the
world Elesin has lost – as David Richards
has rightly observed, a world usually
praised through proverb and metaphor.[10]

Yet neither she herself, her fellow market
women, nor the entire community can ever
be the same. All dancing has stopped, as
there are no drums any more to provide the
rhythms: 'The PRAISE SINGER and DRUMMER
stand on the inside of the semi-circle but the
drum is not used at all. The DRUMMER in-
tones under the PRAISE SINGER's invocations'
(p. 216).

The reason for the drums' silence is
simple: Elesin has undermined the osugbo
drums' function by not following their
instructions concerning his death. They have
determined the action and the exact carrying
out of the ritual for generations, and it was
unthinkable that Elesin would now disobey.
Neither the osugbo drummers nor Olunde
(who is – erroneously – convinced of his

The chorus leader approaches through the foyer into the arena with the corpse of Olunde. Photo: Jan Woollams.

father's death by the correct interpretation of the drums' message) can be expected to reckon with his failure, since this is a new experience for the whole community.

It is logical for Soyinka to emphasize the silence of the osugbo drummers in his stage direction. The talking drum's main task is, as its name indicates, to speak, to transmit messages, to communicate. But Elesin's behaviour has deprived the drums of this function, and they have become useless. The last scene is thus a theatrically brilliant documentation of the breakdown of a formerly harmonious communicative pattern.

In Manchester the envisaged *mise-en-scène* was modified in some crucial, musical respects. Thus, in the last scene the master drummer even advances to the leader of the chorus, slowly approaching through the foyer into the arena with the corpse of Olunde. The script requires no drumming at this point: however, in the RET production Muraina Oyelami plays the melody of the

dirge that is chanted by the women. But although he drums the words 'Ale le le', he does not communicate with his instrument in the same sense as before.

Likewise the drum is employed in two crucial moments of the last act contrary to the author's stage direction: at the moment of the throwing back of the cloth over Olunde's corpse, and after Elesin's suicide. In these two situations the emotional and dramatic effect of the drumming was seen by the director as more important than its communicative aspect, this latter having been shattered by the dramatic action. Phyllida Lloyd: 'We actually use music as a sort of action itself. I'm trying to think of an example: the moment where Iyaloja throws back the cloth over Olunde, and the drum really goes into "batata".'

Through this alteration of the play's ending, which reduces the acoustic contrast with its beginning as suggested in Soyinka's script, the production was deprived of a definite interpretation of the community's future fate. Soyinka's powerful dramaturgic sense of the dichotomy between silence and dirge in the end was to some extent lost in the production – arguably one of its weaker aspects, though it could also be understood as a more optimistic interpretation, since Elesin's failure does not seem to paralyze the others in the way suggested by the author. This would make the play basically a tragedy of Elesin as an individual. If the drums, as the script indicates, were silenced, the whole community would appear to be weakened. Phyllida Lloyd comments:

I think that there is hope at the end of the play. There is hope in the future of the unborn child, undoubtedly. In that sense the play is quite Shakespearean. It's a little bit like the end of *King Lear*, where you feel complete devastation around you, but that one of the forces for good, as it were, remains, to say, 'those of us who stay behind will never see such events again', and you see those people go off into the night and you know that somehow the circle, the wheel will turn and the world will be reborn in some way and will be perhaps wiser. It's kind of carthartic.

Communicating with the Supernatural

While Elesin's lust for the bride at the beginning of the play prepares the ground for the oncoming disastrous events, its turning point or peripeteia happens off-stage, some time after the end of Scene iii or in Scene iv. A closer look at the trance scene may shed some light on how the peripeteia is prepared by the foregoing expressive patterns.

The metaphysical aspect of the nonverbal forms of expression is important. Music as the 'intensive language of transition'[11] and dance as 'the movement of transition'[12] play an essential role within Soyinka's holistic world-view, as the basic means of reaching this transitional state of Elesin's consciousness. The non-verbal forms of expression bring about Elesin's trance and make him dance into Orun, the otherworld.

In the Manchester production, Elesin and the Praise-Singer stand face to face, surrounded by the kneeling market women who perform a vague swaying movement with the upper part of their bodies and their arms, then start chanting the dirge. This choreography is the translation of the 'threnodic essence' in a language of movement, reminding one of an image employed by the author:

In cult funerals, the circle of initiate mourners, an ageless swaying grove of dark pines, raises a chant around a mortar of fire, and words are taken back to their roots, to their original poetic sources when fusion was total and the movement of words was the very passage of music and the dance of images.[13]

The master drummer detaches himself from the musicians, running around Elesin, continuously drumming, forcing dynamics and speed. Here are Muraina Oyelami's comments on this situation:

There was a point when I also joined the crowd and ran around Elesin. All this is preparing him to really get the lift. I mean he was about to fly off, to go to the world beyond. . . . Even in a real situation it's the drummer that makes the dancer become possessed – even the priestess or the priest to that possession. . . . And it will reach a climax where he will just let go.

In the background the audience can hear the osugbo drums. The Horseman and his Praise-Singer start jumping on the spot, panting heavily. That was the most evident divergence from the stage direction, which sees Elesin's dance as one 'of solemn regal motions, each gesture of the body . . . made with solemn finality' (p. 182), though it seems clear that there is no definite way for a trance to 'look'. During this sequence of movement the dialogue starts, and the Praise-Singer changes his identity, at times entranced himself: then he speaks as the dead king.

In trying clearly to outline this change of identity, Phyllida Lloyd fell back on a theatrical trick. As a medium, Badejo spoke in Yoruba and with a guttural voice,[14] while as the Praise-Singer he used his normal voice and the English language. The effect is described by the director:

To an English audience it sounds like a voice from beyond, a voice from another world. It's like a trick in a way. What we are losing is that textual clarity, but I think we're compensating by creating a sense of otherness: We are making contact to the other side, and we're using the Yoruba language as a way of doing that.

When Elesin has fallen completely in trance, he stands motionless. The Praise-Singer, who had mediated verbally a few moments before, now connects the world of the living with the world of the dead by means of gesture: looking at and speaking to his friend, he spreads his arms, the left turned to Elesin, the right pointing to the distant upper world.

As Elesin stands in a trance, the Praise-Singer spreads his arms – one pointing to Elesin, the other to the upper world.

Neither in the playscript nor in the production is there any sign of what is about to happen at the next moment. All seem to be prepared for the sacrifice, including the obviously deeply entranced protagonist. This makes the shock for the audience in the following scene even greater, when Elesin's 'animal bellow' from off is heard: 'Leave me alone!' (p. 201). Then he is himself pushed in by Simon Pilkings, who takes the horseman into custody.

Although most European spectators are unlikely to accept the ritual suicide as a communal necessity, the audience feels with Olunde, the son who 'stands frozen to the spot' (p. 201).

Harmonies and Juxtapositions

The reason for this identification lies in Soyinka's perfect preparation in the trance scene: here, with no hint of the final outcome, the situation is harmonious, the communication on a level of perfect inter-action. Iyaloja's warnings in the opening scene, that Elesin should be aware of the possibility of being too earthbound with his final erotic adventure, have by this time been forgotten. The trance sequence, with its depiction of communal and expressive harmony, has made the spectator feel safe and by that means induces the tragic awareness in the following action.

If we note that the communication of the Yoruba community is – at least in its unspoilt state – basically harmonious, complex, and technically elaborate, the opposite is true for the Europeans. First of all, music and dance in the second and fourth scenes have no aspects of communication but are reduced to status symbols or representation. Secondly the quality of the rendition of these art forms is obviously poor. Thirdly the Europeans are unable to decode the 'native' communication, as Pilkings's helplessness in Scene ii makes apparent.

The contrast is further intensified by the immediacy of the transition. Scene ii opens with music and dance, but the difference between this and what has gone before is only too obvious and reveals its satirical intention. The Pilkingses dance a tango, dressed in sacred Egungun costumes. The music is not rendered live, but comes from an old, hand-cranked gramophone, with its very restricted acoustic qualities. Moreover, the machine doesn't create but merely reproduces the music. The dancers are European, the Tango comes from Argentina, while the costumes are genuinely West African (and, more important, taboo). The contrast between the third and fourth scenes is constructed in a parallel way, and here Soyinka's characterization, scarcely the depiction of a healthy multicultural experiment, makes a satirical comment on colonialist attitudes and the alienation of western culture.

Phyllida Lloyd's *mise-en-scène* took such character contrasts to the verge of absurdism. In the second scene a *rectangular* green carpet is rolled out and covers the yellow circle – 'a kind of rape of the market', as she describes it. The different position of Amusa and Joseph becomes clear in one detail: the houseboy, without fear, steps onto this symbol of European privacy, while the stubborn Sergeant desperately tries to remain standing outside the carpet during the dispute with his master. Yet he is alienated from his culture too: in this situation, as well as during the quarrel with the market women in Scene iii, he stands upright, in an exaggerated military manner. He has internalized the body language of the colonialists.

The contrasts were displayed in the other characters as well – cool but controlled agility, elasticity, and *joie de vivre* for the Yoruba figures, stiff, jerky, and clumsy movements for the Europeans. In the fourth scene a red carpet is rolled out that splits the yellow circle in two halves. A military drum-roll is heard that causes the dancing couples to deploy in one long row to honour the Prince of Wales, who is parading by. All movements are equal, the subjects have become automated: there is no space for any individualism. Phyllida Lloyd comments:

It's like a contrast to Elesin Oba at the beginning with his Praise-Singers. And it was all free and joyful and alive. And then we had our Prince coming in, all stiff and absurd.

The choreography of the Yoruba movements reveals the very opposite – each actor being free to add a personal note to a certain movement that was distinct from the others and mirrors his or her individuality. Yet the audience was aware of the fundamental unity within the group. There was a basic movement pattern, but never a drilled symmetry.

Audience and Reception

For acoustic and logistic reasons, the dialogue that was spoken during the procession around the foyer at the beginning couldn't be understood. Part of the audience had already taken their seats inside, while those spectators who joined the procession could hardly follow the words because of the generalized 'noise'. Inside the arena, the market women obviously gossiped with each other in Yoruba and Pidgin respectively. While the Yoruba language in the trance sequence was used as a way of characterizing the communication between the entranced Praise-Singer and the dead King, the director's intention in this scene didn't focus on language as a tool for developing the plot, but to give a photograph-like impression of an alien culture. In Peter Badejo's words: 'What the audience need to know is to see this life rather than concentrate on what they're saying.' Or as Phyllida Lloyd put it:

I think the reason that they're talking in Yoruba at the beginning when the audience come in is not an attempt to alienate the audience or to confuse them. It's simply trying to create a little bit of a 'fly on a wall' experience for them, so that they're coming into something that really is happening. Those women really are talking in their indigenous languages and relating to each other as characters. And the audience might feel they're part of some real experience. It's not a play – it's actually a slice of life.

The first scene reveals a language that is characterized by its highly poetic style and which is difficult to decode even for people familiar with the English language. Soyinka skilfully gives a theatrical translation in the second scene by showing the Pilkingses, who are not able to interpret the drum messages and thus depend on the information of Amusa and Joseph. It was this theatrical translation that made the director think of an unconventional *mise-en-scène*:

If I'd had any time with Soyinka beforehand, I would have said, 'Why don't we perform that whole opening scene in Yoruba?' Because then the audience will stop trying to decode it. And they will relax as they would if they were watching an opera. Or if they went to Nigeria and were watching a procession go past. They would be thinking, they would be trying to read it, and they'd be saying, 'Oh, it's a celebration of something.' And: 'This man is getting married.' And then in the second scene it becomes clearer what is happening.

Bearing in mind the never-ending debate about the use of European languages in

The exaggerated, military stance of the Sergeant, alienated from his own culture, during the quarrel with the market women in Scene iii.

African drama, it appears almost paradoxical that a European director should consider translating a whole scene back from English into Yoruba. But bilingualism as it was employed in the trance scene was dramatically very effective, and Phyllida Lloyd surely correct in her claim that the main information of the first scene – the festival atmosphere and the marriage of Elesin – would be conveyed even if played in Yoruba. Yet it's likely that Soyinka's intention was precisely to show the richness of the language, the multitude of variations, the proverbs, the flamboyant images, rather than to develop the plot.

Lloyd's reference to the 'fly on the wall experience' implies, with respect to the audience, a realistic but distanced intention. For African theatre, African life and thinking, are still too alien for participation: first, one cannot do more than observe. And even that can be shocking, as Peter Badejo recalls in a wry recollection of the beginning of the show:

It's new to them! The first day, the moment they heard drums, people started running helter-skelter for their seats! But as time goes on, some of them are beginning to relax and just enjoy it outside before they go in. But again, it might be the first time in their life they will have seen this kind of theatre, starting that way.

Problems of an 'Extended Mise-en-Scène'

The dirge in the play is a musical detail that caused some misunderstanding within the company. Badejo hinted at the fact that some of the (European) actors interpreted the dirge as a sad melody, akin to the conventions of European church music – composed in a minor key. The dirge in Manchester, however, revealed a melody basing on a major triad. Although the melody goes down, it doesn't sound like a motif of a requiem. As Gerhard Kubik has shown, it is unusual in African music to express feelings by harmonic patterns.[15] In his words, most indigenous African music is described as 'emotionally neutral'.

67

Phyllida Lloyd and Muraina Oyelami stressed the concessions made in the production to European acoustic habits. As the verbal nature of the talking drum cannot be perceived by a western audience (or even by some of the actors involved), the verbal stimulus has to be transformed into a musical stimulus to be acknowledged by the spectators as a hint to a certain action. Phyllida Lloyd gives an example from the first scene:

Sometimes we have bridged the gap between the talking drum and western understanding. . . . And I might have said, 'You know, that sound needs to be much more important. It needs to draw the attention much more.' Whether that means it needs to be louder or it needs to be longer or have more contrast with what's just come before, I don't legislate on that. But what I just said is, that as a punctuation mark it's not drawing my attention. There is a moment where Elesin sees the bride the first time, and they all go 'ahhh', and the talking drum comments on that. We worked quite hard to try and give that its full value. At first nobody even noticed her. It just wasn't enough. And now, we've actually the whole company looking to her.

As can be seen, to achieve the intended effect on the audience the lack of intercultural understanding has to be compensated for by the quality of the acoustic stimulus. This wasn't the only compromise of the production: as I mentioned earlier, music was in some parts used as an emotional or dramatic booster. Yet the production could in no ways be regarded as a display of unreflected exotism.

The biggest challenge for the *mise-en-scène* was to create a homogenous work from a heterogenous team that had never worked together before. Soyinka's plays not only demand technically well-trained and highly specialized artists as musicians, dancers, drummers, etc., but need to be understood in their metaphysical dimension. The task of the director therefore is to integrate the various levels of expression in the play as well as the different personal backgrounds of the artists.

According to Phyllida Lloyd, a basic problem in Manchester was that the actors were unequally experienced in the language and metaphysics of the play. Peter Badejo is a brilliant dancer and choreographer, familiar with the Yoruba metaphysics – but he lacked the actors' training and experience, and had to struggle with the complex English language, while the other participants had the opposite problem.

Although Phyllida Lloyd expressed her difficulties mainly as concerened with the dualism of dialogue and metaphysics, these existed on other levels. The dance and music of the Yoruba culture were as alien to her as they were to the other actors of the ensemble, and this was likely to have an effect on her role as a co-ordinator of the various levels. Although thanks to Badejo and Oyelami she could rely on specialist help, her ability to control the correctness of the communicative pattern in its totality was limited, since she herself was only partly familiar with Soyinka's theatrical language. She agreed that in some crucial cases she was uncertain about what the drum was actually saying.

The lack of co-ordination between the different expressive levels as a consequence of intercultural misunderstanding became obvious in one detail, which accidentally emerged during my interviews. When Joseph is asked for a translation of the drums' message by Pilkings in Scene ii, David Webber, who played the Houseboy and is not himself a Yoruba, reacted with a gesture of obviously trying to listen to the direction of the drums. Yet Joseph's answer concerning the ambiguity of the drums' message was a contradiction to his own gesture of listening, as of Oyelami's drumming in this moment, since the latter was beating a completely regular and unambiguous rhythm (for Yoruba speakers). This detail, unimportant though it may seem, reveals the complicated structures of multicultural communication and the consequences which may follow in the staging of a play where this needs to be conveyed.

Patterns of Communication

In *Death and the King's Horseman*, Wole Soyinka sets up a pattern of communication that consists of three elements: words, music, and dance. In production, the ideal would be a well-balanced equality, a system where each of the Yoruba communicants is able to speak and understand on different levels, by contrast with the static expressive nature of the European representatives – for whom music and dance are either 'noise' or luxury, but never a tool for communication.

The Europeans thus become the dramaturgical vehicles for creating comic relief. By showing this contrasting communicative pattern, Soyinka develops and displays the tragic action, through which the breakdown of the protagonist has its cruel impact on his community, where it is mirrored by the loss of some of the expressive levels. The relation of each of these expressive levels to one another provides, then, the motor of the dramatic conflict.

Every non-Yoruba audience will necessarily realize that they can understand only a part of the overall structure of communication. What is crucial is not a complete understanding but a perception of the relation between the communicative elements and its shifts. This is even possible for people unfamiliar with the Yoruba culture.

The basic difficulty for a western theatre is to find the specialists necessary for a successful staging of *Death and the King's Horseman*. It is not sufficient to have actors 'playing' dancers or musicians: they have to *be* dancers or musicians, knowing the aesthetics of such African communicative patterns as 'call-and-response' or 'vital aliveness', and they have finally to reject the notion that communication is primarily a matter of speech.

If a theatre is lucky enough to find the specialists, it is the task of the *mise-en-scène* to develop the various expressive elements in such a way that the multiple dialogue becomes the basic structure of the dramatic action. The RET production in fact succeeded in realizing the concept described by Peter Badejo:

Every Yoruba man or African believes in the total utility of the medium of communication. And that's the easiest way I can put it: total utility of the medium of communication.

Notes and References

1. Hanna Scolnicov, 'Theatre Space, Theatrical Space, and the Theatrical Space Without', in *Themes in Drama, Vol. IX: The Theatrical Space*, ed. James Redmond (Cambridge, 1987), p. 22.

2. See D. Fraser, ed., *The Royal Exchange Theatre Company: an Illustrated Record* (Manchester, 1988), p. 22.

3. Wole Soyinka, 'Who's Afraid of Elesin Oba?', in *Wole Soyinka, Art, Dialogue, and Outrage: Essays on Literature and Culture*, ed. Biodun Jeyifo (Ibadan, 1988), p. 116.

4. Ibid., p. 39.

5. Wole Soyinka, *Death and the King's Horseman*, in *Six Plays* (London: Methuen, 1984), p. 146. All further quotations and the page numbers indicated in the text are taken from this edition.

6. According to R. F. Thompson, 'vital aliveness' and 'vitality' are basic aesthetic categories of African dance. See his *African Art in Motion: Icon and Act* (Los Angeles; Berkeley; London, 1974), p. 7 and 9.

7. See, for example, J. N. Amankulor, 'Ekpe Festival as Religious Ritual and Dance Drama', in *Drama and Theatre in Nigeria*, ed. Yemi Ogunbiyi (Lagos, 1981), p.113-29. Amankulor's depiction of this festival reveals remarkable parallels to the Manchester production concerning spatial structure, the importance of the circle, movement, direction, and content (the importance of a ritual sacrifice for the welfare of the community).

8. R. F. Thompson, op. cit., p. 27.

9. These are not to be mistaken with the drummers in the secret place 'Osugbo'. The drummers on stage (i.e., the 'market drummers') are hired by Elesin and play mainly for the celebration itself, while the osugbo-players are in charge for the correct timing of the ritual.

10. David Richards, 'Owe l'esin oro, Proverbs like Horses: Wole Soyinka's *Death and the King's Horseman*', in *Journal of Commonwealth Literature*, XIX, No. 1 (1984), p. 95.

11. Wole Soyinka, *Myth, Literature, and the African World* (Cambridge, 1976), p. 36.

12. Obi Maduakor, *Wole Soyinka: an Introduction to his Writing* (New York, 1986), p. 269.

13. Wole Soyinka, 'The Fourth Stage', in *Myth, Literature, and the African World*, op. cit., p. 147.

14. A guttural voice as indicating a supernatural being is a common phenomenon in African ritual. See, for instance, Edward Lifschitz, 'Hearing is Believing: Acoustic Aspects of Masking in Africa', in *West African Masks and Cultural Systems*, ed. S. L. Kasfir (Tervuren, 1988), p. 221-9.

15. Gerhard Kubik, 'Verstehen in afrikanischen Musikkulturen', in *Musik in Afrika*, ed. Artur Simon (Museum für Völkerkunde Berlin, 1983), p. 322-3.

Caroline Gardiner

From Bankside to the West End: a Comparative View of London Audiences

The received wisdom regarding the composition of the audience for Shakespeare's theatre has shifted in accordance with the social assumptions of the times – from Alfred Harbage's assertion of a popular, homogeneous audience, evolved for the egalitarian 'forties, to Ann Jennalie Cook's argument for a 'privileged' audience, put forward in the elitist 'eighties. While Andrew Gurr's *Playgoing in Shakespeare's London* corrects the worst excesses of both views, it remains dependent upon a great deal of inference from inadequate documentation, often directed to other purposes, and sometimes upon necessary guesswork, however rooted in common-sense. Caroline Gardiner teaches and researches in the Department of Arts Policy and Management at City University, whence have emerged the most detailed attempts to 'profile' the theatregoing populace of contemporary London: and here she suggests that some of the approaches and even the findings of modern audience researchers may shed new light on the controversy. Sometimes the results are surprising – and include the possibility that, relative to the pool of population available, theatre is now actually a more popular activity than in Shakespeare's London. However, she concludes that, overall, the percentage attending the theatre has remained remarkably constant, and constantly low.

STATISTICAL SURVEYS of audiences for theatre in England have become common-place. The audience member is increasingly accustomed to arriving at her or his seat to discover a questionnaire placed upon it. Typical theatre audience surveys currently attempt to define basic demographic pro-files such as age, sex, and home area. The information collected is usually destined either to be used in theatre marketing, or to be submitted to funding bodies as part of a grant application.

Audience surveys in England began to appear as a regular feature of theatregoing from the early 1970s onwards. Early surveys drew directly on market research techniques developed by social scientists in the universities. Indeed, the first audience survey to be given wide circulation was conducted by the university sociologist Dr. Peter Mann in 1966, at Sheffield Playhouse. [1]

Prior to this, statistical information about audiences was not readily available. The theatre scholar, in forming a picture of the theatre audience of the past, had to rely on documentation surviving from the relevant period. Such documents relating to English theatre history largely consist of managers' account and receipt books, and of contemporary personal accounts of theatregoing. But the theatre manager of the nineteenth century and earlier was, quite naturally, interested primarily in attendances and receipts. There was usually no particular reason why he (or occasionally she) should wish to keep any record of who was attending the theatre, in addition to how many.

A systematic interest in who is attending becomes more evident following the advent of large-scale and centrally administered public funding of the arts. Although this did exist prior to the foundation of the Arts Council of Great Britain in 1946, this date is often taken as the starting point for arts funding in Britain becoming a major area of both government and public concern. When public money is being distributed in an apparently structured way, it has tended to provoke discussion about the equity of such distribution.

In the Arts Council's Charter of Incorporation of 1967 three objects are outlined, the second being 'to increase the accessibility of the arts to the public throughout Great Britain'. Accessibility is often used interchangeably with availability by arts managers, as if a widespread provision of theatres and performances is in itself a sufficient answer to potential charges of unjust distribution. But the idea that there must be seen to be social justice in the way theatre is funded through the public purse does manifest itself as a demand for a demographically wide-ranging audience, rather than simply a geographical spread of theatres.

Audience Profiles and their Purposes

The distribution of theatre buildings, and the justice or otherwise of that distribution may be relatively easily determined. Determining the profile of an audience inevitably calls for specialized research. It was not until the rapid growth of departments of social sciences within the universities in the 1960s, with the consequent increasing expertise in the techniques of demographic profiling in the academic sector, that audience surveys really began on any large scale. Fragmentary published survey results from individual venues exist from the 1960s, and audience surveys proliferated rapidly from the early 1970s.

Theatre audience surveys usually attempt to define the audience in a quantifiable way. They do not often explore the audience response to a performance – something that is difficult to quantify. This apparent exclusion of the aesthetic dimension makes such research appear understandably distasteful to many theatre practitioners. But current audience research tends to concentrate on statistically based definitions of audiences, such as age, sex, and home area, since this provides the quickest means to acquire information for use in marketing or in negotiations with funding bodies.

If audience profiles are requested by a funding body, then the results may be used to measure how well the audience matches up to the expressed policy of that funding body in the type and mix of audiences it

is giving priority to. For example, does the audience contain a good mix of social classes? The implications of this mix are seldom addressed by a survey, the aim being to demonstrate how the theatre is performing in meeting target audience profiles.

The position is complicated by the fact that often the desired mix is not specified by the funding body. Would 10 per cent of the audience being unemployed be considered a 'fair' social mix? Survey results can be valuable in this area, in monitoring clearly expressed policies: for example, if a theatre's policy is that it should cater mainly for those people who do not go to the theatre very often, then a survey is one way of checking the effectiveness of that policy.

Although theatre audience research may often be undertaken because of a perceived need to establish audience profiles in order to justify public funding, in fact survey results are commonly consigned to the theatre's marketing department. A typical use of such results would be to discover which newspapers the regular theatregoers read most often, and to concentrate advertising primarily on those newspapers in the future. Interest in the long-term audience mix for philosophical reasons is often subordinated to the pragmatic requirements of selling tickets in the immediate future. This is understandable – but regrettable, since theatres need to look to maintaining their audiences in the future.

There have been attempts to define what many arts managers would consider a far more important aspect of audience profiles than their age or sex – what they think about the production. Structured group discussions led by market researchers are used in drawing out the opinions and concerns of a group of people chosen to represent a spectrum of the public, ranging from non-theatregoers to dedicated theatregoers. A perennial cry of arts managers after undertaking a statistical audience survey is 'Yes, very interesting, but it doesn't tell me why people *aren't* coming.' Group discussion research may do so, but it will not usually provide solutions.

It is hard to see how the theatre manager can act on knowing that many of the local community do not attend the theatre because their gardens take too much time. This was the response of several people in such a research group which was commissioned from National Opinion Polls in 1981.[2] And how is a theatre manager to respond to the assertion, also from the NOP study, that 'I want to go somewhere I can drive or walk to rather than have the hassle of trying to park in the West End. So when we go to the theatre, we usually go to the National Theatre.'[3] Such responses can be disappointing and frustrating for the theatre manager. Audience research, of whatever type, will not provide a conclusive answer to the fundamental question: what makes people choose to go to the theatre or to stay away?

So in spite of the apparent wider interest in audience profiles for reasons of debate about theatre and its role in society, and in how that role should be publicly funded, audience research is now often collected for much the same reasons as early theatre managers kept receipt and account books – to find out what is successful, and how to create more ticket sales. However, while pragmatic motives may have prevailed, now and in the past, this is not to exclude the possibility of a critical and philosophical analysis of information about audience profiles both present and past by the theatre scholar. By comparing approaches to this area of research, this paper seeks to outline differences and similarities not only in audience profiles but also in the ways in which audiences have featured in the critical analysis of theatre in different periods.

Contemporary and Shakespearean

The period of English theatre history which has received the largest amount of scholarly attention is that of Elizabethan and Jacobean theatre, and the theatre of Shakespeare in particular. In the present day, the largest survey of theatre audience profiles in England is that conducted on the West End theatre in London by the Department of Arts Policy and Management at City University, London. While accepting that the data available about theatre audiences in Shakespeare's London and those in present-day London had been collected and collated for very different reasons, this paper attempts a broad comparison between what is known about audiences for theatre in London in Shakespeare's time and in the present day.

The concern of the Shakespearean scholar of audiences will be primarily the illumination Shakespeare's texts through an analysis of his likely audience. Those of the researcher into audiences of the present day will be largely how to apply the information collected to the practical management of theatre, particularly in encouraging future audiences.

The major research sources on which this paper draws for its analysis of the present-day London theatre audiences are three large-scale audience survey programmes conducted in the West End by City University between 1982 and 1991. The audience surveys involved self-completion questionnaires being issued at around 90 different productions, with approximately 30,000 theatregoers participating over the ten year span of the survey period.

For Shakespeare's audience, there are three major academic works which the researcher on theatre audiences will draw on – Alfred Harbage's *Shakespeare's Audience*, Ann Jennalie Cook's *The Privileged Playgoers of Shakespeare's London, 1576-1642*, and Andrew Gurr's *Playgoing in Shakespeare's London*.[4] Harbage attempts an analysis both of how many people attended Shakespeare's theatre, and of who they were. Cook is mainly concerned with refuting Harbage's conclusion that Shakespeare's plays attracting a socially wide-ranging audience. Although she does not attempt to put a precise figure on the size of Shakespeare's audience, she does give a detailed analysis of playhouse sizes, and the size of the population of London, and some links can be made between the two. Cook's priority remains *who* rather than *how many*.

Gurr's book attempts a synthesis of the two previous accounts. In his view, while

Harbage may have gone too far in his insistence on a popular audience, Cook gives too narrow an account of the likely audience, as the title of her book indeed suggests. Gurr does not attempt a numerical analysis of the size of the audience, although he does note that 'between the 1560s, when the first purpose built playhouses were established, and 1624, when all playhouses were closed, well over fifty million visits were made to playhouses'.[5] He does not offer an account of how this figure of fifty million was arrived at, but it is presumably based on lists of theatres which are known to have existed, playhouse capacities, as far as they are known, and information from managers' receipt books as to typical percentages of capacities achieved.

In profiling the likely contemporary audience for Shakespeare's plays, Gurr concentrates on a detailed analysis of such external factors as physical conditions in the playhouses and social conditions in London at the time. Like Cook, his primary concern is with *who*, rather than *how many*. In the absence of comprehensive records of attendances, any account of how many people attended Shakespeare's theatre must be at best a very rough estimate.

The relative paucity of research on Shakespeare's audiences, compared with the huge amount of scholarly literature in other areas of Shakespearian studies, indicates both the intrinsic difficulties of obtaining suitable source material for such research, and the relatively low priority given to audience studies in historical theatre research. Each of the three books cited in turn draws on three main sources for their analysis – the plays themselves and the internal evidence they offer, the surviving receipt and account books of the theatre managers, and contemporary documents and letters which deal with the theatre.

Cook points out that what is considered common knowledge about audiences is often thought not worth recording. This may regrettably have been the case with contemporary comment on the composition of Shakespeare's audience. It is certainly the case that much of the audience research

conducted in the present day tends to confirm previously expressed views of how theatre audiences are made up. Any analysis of the composition of Shakespeare's audience has to take into account the possibility that what is commented on in contemporary documents is only the exceptional.

For the present London theatre audience, we have a large amount of data on day-to-day audience profiles. Often results from this will seem to the reader like stating the obvious. The Shakespearean scholar can thus only bemoan the probability that the obvious was not thought worth stating in Shakespeare's day. The lack of precise audience data from the Elizabethan and Jacobean periods, and the different methodologies by which the data was recorded then and in the present day, does mean that precise comparisons cannot be made between the two audiences. However, general observations about apparent similarities and differences between the two are possible.

Profiling West End Audiences

I shall look first at the background to the recent research on theatre audiences in London. In 1982, the Department of Arts Policy and Management at City University, where I teach and research, was invited by the Society of West End Theatre to carry out the first ever full-scale survey of audiences for London theatres. SWET is a trade association which represents theatres, managements, and producers in the area of London broadly known as the 'West End', although in fact a number of theatres such as Sadlers Wells, which lie outside this area, are members of the Society. Its membership includes around 50 theatres, both grant-aided and commercial, but not London theatres which might generally be described as fringe or pub theatres.

While SWET membership cannot be considered fully synonymous with 'London theatre', the terms 'London theatre' and 'West End theatre' are both used to describe SWET member theatres in this paper. A smaller update survey was carried out in 1985 and

1986, and a full-scale survey again in 1990 and 1991.

The research took the form of audience surveys of the now familiar type: audience members were given a self-completion questionnaire asking them to give a range of information about themselves – standard questions to determine social profile (such as age, sex, home area), and questions about theatregoing habits and aspects of their current visit. Information on current London audiences for the plays of Shakespeare in particular was obtained through surveys of the Royal Shakespeare Company at its Barbican and Pit theatres (and at the Aldwych when the company was based there), and for Shakespeare productions at the Royal National Theatre, together with the occasional commercial productions of Shakespeare in the West End.

In the case of the West End theatres, the audience research was driven mainly by marketing and public relations needs rather than by the concern to demonstrate audience reach to any public funding body. Prior to the research in 1982, it was widely assumed that the West End was very heavily dependent on overseas tourism for its audience. Whenever the level of overseas tourism to Britain fell, there was inevitably a rash of 'death of the West End' press stories. For example, Bernard Levin had written in the *Sunday Times* in January 1978 :

The London theatre would drop dead overnight if the foreigners stopped coming; indeed it would not long survive if there were any substantial diminution in their numbers, and it would take only a hiccup in the world's currency exchange values or a threatening cloud over its international relations for many foreigners . . . to decide to stay at home.'[6]

West End managements feared that this could lead to a crisis of confidence among theatre producers and owners, becoming a self-fulfilling prophecy: thus, if local people thought that shows in the West End were in danger of imminent closure, they might consider theatre in London not worth bothering to visit. A structured audience research programme would allow the West End managers to see changes in audience numbers and profiles for their own productions in the context of the West End overall, and to plan on the basis of either trying to fill the gaps in their audience by aiming for the kinds of people they were not already attracting, or by trying to encourage further attendances among their current audiences.

In the event, Levin's article proved to have overestimated the importance of the overseas audience. Both fluctuations in world currency exchange values and threatening clouds over international relations have occurred since the article was written, and the West End theatre has weathered both. Because of the research programme, it has been possible for West End managers to assess the effects of such crises, and as the survey programme progressed and a data series was established over time, to predict and be prepared for the likely effect of current events.

Some Points of Comparison

There are several points of similarity between Shakespeare's theatre and the present West End theatre which make them particularly suitable for comparison. Firstly, the West End theatres are now run on a largely commercial basis, as indeed was Shakespeare's theatre. In neither case does a commercial motive exclude a genuine interest in the drama, and the membership of SWET does include companies, such as the Royal Shakespeare Company and the National Theatre, in receipt of public subsidy.

Secondly, although present-day productions of Shakespeare inevitably carry some association with the preservation of cultural heritage, if any theatre now can be considered 'popular', as scholars such as Harbage have claimed Shakespeare's theatre was, it is theatre in the West End of London. Around 11.3 million tickets were sold for the fifty West End theatres in the period from April 1990 to 1991, the period covered by the most recent major audience profile survey. For theatres outside London, numbering over three hundred, the estimated figure is 13.4 million for the same period.[7]

Since the West End is commercial, then it is likely that the repertory will be designed primarily to meet audience demand rather than to shape it. It seems likely that the same would have been the case with theatres in Shakespeare's time, though writers such as Ben Jonson would have considered that they had an important role in shaping public taste. As Gurr points out: 'Every time Jonson called his audience "spectators", as he almost invariably did, he was covertly sneering at the debased preference for stage spectacle rather than the poetic "soul" of the play.'[8]

Thirdly, London as a centre in Shakespeare's time was a magnet for business, educational, and legal affairs, with a large concentration of wealthly individuals – and continues to play this role in the present day. One crucial point of difference, however, is that the concentration of theatres in London in Shakespeare's time, according to Cook, was a direct response to the concentration of a leisured elite in the capital, whereas today London's theatres are responsible for drawing many people to the capital solely to visit them.

Entertainment tourism is thus a major source of revenue for the capital city. In the twelve-month period covered by the 1990-91 SWET audience survey report, audiences visiting West End theatres spent around £114 million in addition to ticket purchases on items associated with theatregoing, such as travel and eating out locally. This is only around £70 million less than they spent on West End theatre tickets during the same twelve months.

Turning to a consideration of research methods, the major difficulty for the researcher using contemporary accounts of Shakespeare's audience is that the surviving documents will often offer only a partial view. Thus, many are polemics against the theatres themselves, and are driven by a fear that young people will become corrupted as a result of their contact with those who frequent the theatres.

Whereas at our Comon Playse and such lyke Exercises whiche be comonly exposed to be seene

for money, everye lewd persone thinketh himselfe (for his penny) worthye of the chiefe and most comodious place withoute respecte of any other, either for age or estimacion in the comon weale, which bringeth the youthe to such an impudente famyliarite with theire betters that often tymes greite contempte of Maisters, Parents, and Magistrats followeth thereof.[9]

Concern is expressed that the theatre audience is drawn from too wide a spectrum of society, and contemporary comment on Shakespeare's audience was often concerned with the social and moral questions arising from this apparently undesirable audience composition.

The partiality of such documents may well provide a source of amusement to the present-day researcher, since theatre in London, and in the West End in particular, has been considered by its critics to be unacceptable today for precisely the opposite reason cited by contemporary critics of Shakespearean theatre – that is, that its audiences are too exclusively middle and upper class. Social and moral questions of audience composition have been important issues in both the periods under consideration, and contemporary audience research has been used in the service of discussion of such issues.

Methodology of the Modern Surveys

While the main methodological problem for the researcher on Elizabethan theatre is how to disentangle the existing evidence from its context, the main problem facing the present-day researcher on audiences is how to collect the original evidence in such a way that it provides a reliable profile of the audience. This means adhering to the best practices of market research, and in particular accurate sampling. In the case of the West End theatre, obtaining a representative sample of a whole range of theatre audiences across more than fifty theatres with enough confidence to say that it was possible to profile a 'West End theatre audience' proved to be a daunting task.

The first West End survey programme in 1981 began with a series of pilot surveys at a range of different plays and shows. As well as testing out questionnaire design and survey method, the aim of the pilot was to establish whether day of the week or type of production resulted in greater variations in audience profile. It was not possible at the pilot stage to test accurately for the effects of seasonal variations, since that would have meant too long a testing period.

The pilot surveys showed that in certain key aspects of audience profile, such as age, sex, home area, and frequency of theatre-going, the type of production being surveyed was a better predictor of audience profile than day of the week, and that variations in audience for the same show on different days of the week were relatively minor. With this in mind, a survey programme was designed to test specifically for the effects of variations in type of production on audience profile.

It was not possible to keep day of the week as a constant throughout the survey period. Ten basic types of production were identified as representing the range of shows on in the West End: modern drama, comedy, modern or pop musical, traditional musical, revue or variety, dance, opera or operetta, children's shows or pantomime, thriller, and classical play. If an example of each of these had been surveyed on the same day of ten successive weeks, then seasonal variations might have begun to have an effect.

The pilot surveys had shown that audience profiles of the same show varied very little between Tuesday, Wednesday, and Thursday evenings. A series of ten surveys was therefore designed to take place over three and half weeks, one for each type of show, on Tuesday to Thursday evenings. This set of ten surveys was then repeated at different points during the calendar year, using where possible the same shows in each set of surveys. In addition, two long-running shows were selected specifically to test for seasonal variations in audience profile, and these were surveyed several times during the year, always on the same day of the week. A similar series of surveys tested for day of the week variations by

surveying the same show for at least four performances in one week, repeated at several points during the year.

A Jigsaw of Information

In this way, the research project built up a jigsaw of information about West End theatre audiences according to a number of variables. The approach was a pragmatic one towards dealing with the problem of obtaining a 'representative' sample of the West End audience across more than 1,800 performances at more than 50 theatres annually. However, when the survey had been completed, it became clear that it was necessary both for public relations and marketing purposes to attempt to produce some kind of aggregated figures which would allow people to talk about who the 'West End audience' might be.

The survey results made it clear that variations in production were by far the most consistent and significant variables in audience profile. Day of the week variations were relatively minor, and seasonal variations were mainly in the percentage of the audience who were from overseas. The main message of the surveys was therefore that it is the play, show, or musical that people tend to go for, and that each type tends to attract its own kind of audience.

Parallel to the audience survey, City University had begun to collect, for the first time, detailed box office figures weekly for every theatre in the West End. It was therefore now possible to state accurately what proportion of seats had been sold for which type of show. An aggregated set of results for those surveys which had been testing for variations in type of production could therefore be weighted according to what proportion of ticket sales had in fact gone to each type, in order to give a reasonable assessment of the profile of 'the West End audience'.

When this was done, it was discovered that the results produced figures very close to those which could be externally verified. For example, it was possible to tell from the box-office survey how many tickets had been sold through ticket agencies, and how many through SWET's half-price ticket booth in Leicester Square. In both cases, the actual percentage of sales made by these methods was very close to the figures produced by the aggregated weighted results.

The surveys have been carried out in the West End on a five-yearly basis since 1981, and each time the audience profile by type of production has shown strong similarities, even with a ten-year lapse. The profile of the West End audience, therefore, will be largely dependent on the balance of types of production in any given year. While the methodology required for our present-day research into audiences is far more complex than that applied to the study of Shakespeare's audience, it will be clear that both demand a painstaking scrutiny of the data available if a definition of the 'audience' is to be attempted,

Problems of Periodization

When looking at accounts of Shakespeare's audience, there remains the problem of defining the period of Shakespearean theatre to look at. Is it the whole period during which Shakespeare himself was active as a playwright, or perhaps that when he was with the King's Men at the Globe? The Elizabethan period only, or also the Jacobean? It is difficult to define with precision what we might mean by Shakespeare's theatre, and if we are to define the audience for that theatre, it is necessary that we make some attempt to define our period of study.

The three academic texts cited all take different stands on the proper period of enquiry, which makes any synthesis of their views problematic. Harbage covers a much more restricted period of time than the other two, dealing mainly with the period 1592 to 1613 in his general analysis of Shakespeare's audience. This covers roughly the period during which there is general scholarly consensus that Shakespeare wrote all his extant plays.

In pinning down a percentage of the population of London who went to the theatre, Harbage acknowledges that this would change from year to year with available theatre capacity and increases in the population of London. The latter figure was subject to particularly rapid change during Shakespeare's lifetime. He therefore selects one year, 1605, for the calculation of the percentage of Londoners who actually attended Shakespeare's theatre.

Cook's period of analysis is quite explicit, and is contained in the title of her book, *The Privileged Playgoers of Shakespeare's London 1576-1642* – that is, the period from the opening of Burbage's Theatre to the closure of the theatres by Parliament. Since she is concerned primarily with *who* went to the theatre rather than with precise estimates of how many, much of her book is concentrated on documentation and analysis of the social context during this period. It is not her aim to produce a percentage figure for theatregoing by Londoners in the way that Harbage attempts, and therefore her period of study can be wider.

Gurr takes his period of analysis further back than Cook. He covers the period from 1567, when the Red Lion playhouse was built by Burbage's brother-in-law and partner John Brayne, up to 1642. Like Cook, Gurr's enquiry is largely focused on social context, and in particular on the changes in the audience profile which might relate to that social context during the period of enquiry. His study is therefore broader in scope than the other two, and, as with Cook, there is no attempt to pin down a figure for the likely size of the audience at a specific point in time.

This paper will therefore offer a numerical comparison between Harbage's estimate of the percentage of Londoners who went to the theatre in Shakespeare's time and the percentage who attend in the present day, and a more general comparison of both Cook's and Gurr's analysis of London theatre audience profiles during the period 1567-1642 with the most recent audience profiles in the West End.

The definition of the period to be considered when looking at the present-day audience is much easier. Each of the three major surveys conducted since 1981 has taken a snapshot of the audience over a period of one calendar year, so that seasonal variations have been taken into account in reaching a definition of 'the audience for London theatre'. The surveys have shown relatively little variation in the audience profile over this period. In discussing the London theatre audience in this paper, therefore, the results of the 1990-91 audience survey are used, and these also give a reasonably accurate profile of the audience throughout the 1980s .

Comparisons of Size

I shall look firstly at a comparison between the actual size of the theatre audience in London in Shakespeare's time and the present day. Ticket sales and receipts in themselves do not give an accurate measure of the likely size of the audience. The same number of ticket sales could represent either a few people visiting the theatre many times or many people going a few times. Information on the individual frequency of theatregoing is necessary to make an accurate assessment of the actual number of people attending.

In Harbage's analysis of the size of Shakespeare's audience, he made use of those remaining managers' receipt books which give details of revenues, of reconstructions of the playhouses which give some idea of likely capacities, and contemporary information on numbers of playhouses in London. Using this data, Harbage estimated the number of weekly attendances in 1605 at around 21,000. He then obtained an estimate of the population of London, to include the city, its outer wards and parishes, and outlying districts such as Westminster and Islington, through a refinement of previous estimates. Harbage puts the figure in 1605 around 160,000, though he acknowledges that some scholars would put the figure as high as 220,000.

Using Harbage's 160,000 estimate produces a figure of 13 per cent of the population of London attending the theatre in London in one week in 1605.[10] Harbage does, however, acknowledge that calculation of an accurate percentage figure is dependent on having information about the average frequency of theatregoing by audience members. Weekly attendance may be an over-estimate of the Jacobean devotion to theatregoing. If people went less frequently than this, but with the same number of weekly admissions as Harbage has calculated, then the number of Londoners visiting the theatre, and consequently the percentage of London's population who attended, would be much higher than 13 per cent. Conversely, if the typical audience member was a very frequent theatregoer, seeing individual plays more than once, and attending more than once a week then fewer people, and a much smaller percentage of the population of London than 13 per cent, would have to attend in order to produce the same number of admissions.

Harbage's own observation that attendances were much higher when a new play opened, as compared with later in its run, tends to support the theory that the audience consisted of a small number of people in search of novelty in their theatregoing. If all theatregoers really did go to the theatre once a week in 1605, then 13 per cent of the population of London went to the theatre. If all theatregoers went twice a week, then the percentage figure would be halved to 6.5 per cent, and if all theatregoers attended only once a fortnight, the percentage doubles to 26 per cent. It is clear from this assessment how crucial an accurate measure of average frequency is in assessing a reliable figure for the percentage of London's population who attended the theatre.

Cook concludes, by means of analysis of social factors such as timing of performances in relation to the working hours of different sections of society, and prices of tickets in comparison with average wages, that audiences for Shakespeare would consist primarily of the educated, privileged, and relatively leisured classes. Her interest in establishing attendance figures is therefore primarily in demonstrating that what she calls the privileged playgoers – 'the closest equivalent contemporary term would be "gentleman"'[11] – were sufficient in number to sustain the theatres, without having to broaden the scope of the audience to include lower-class men and women.

Her estimate of likely weekly attendance is close to Harbage's. In 1599, she estimates daily attendance of between 3,000 and 4,000, rising to just over 4,000 in 1609 following the opening of the winter headquarters of the King's Men at Blackfriars.[12] It would seem reasonable to compromise on a figure of around 3,500 daily in 1605, or 21,000 weekly (assuming six performances a week on average, with Sundays excluded). This estimated weekly attendance figure is the same as Harbage's, and like him Cook supports at least weekly theatregoing as typical on the grounds of the relatively rapid turnover of even the most popular plays, suggesting a frequent theatregoing audience which is rapidly exhausted.[13]

Cook's estimate of the population of London is wider in range than Harbage's, between 150,000 in 1576 and 350,000 by 1642. While population growth within this period did not proceed at an even pace, if we were to assume that it did, in the interests of obtaining an estimate of the likely population in 1605 to tie in with Cook's figures, we arrive at a population of around 238,000. Cook does not specify how she has defined 'London' when assessing the population, and she has drawn on a number of different sources in making her estimate.[14]

With attendances, then, of around 21,000 weekly, against an average frequency of theatregoing of about once a week, this would mean that, according to Cook's figures, around 9 per cent of the population of London went to the theatre. Since her estimates of weekly attendances and average frequency of theatregoing are close to those given by Harbage, the difference between their estimates is due to differing assessments of the population of London at the period. Cook estimates the percentage of London's population who fell into her definition of privileged at between 15 per cent and 18 per cent.[15] She thus offers support for her view that the privileged would have been sufficient in number to support the London theatre in 1605 if at least

half of their numbers went to the theatre around once a week.

Assessing the Popularity of Playgoing

Gurr does not attempt to place a figure on the percentage of the population attending the theatre in Shakespeare's time. His book is concerned mainly with demonstrating, through an analysis of contemporary evidence, that Cook's thesis presents too narrow a view of Shakespeare's audience. He would, however, probably not go as far as Harbage in asserting that the audience was a 'popular' one. As he points out in the introduction to this book, 'Harbage [was] working in the 1930s and 1940s when the political climate encouraged him to identify Shakespeare as a truly "popular" playwright appealing to a whole and united nation.'[16]

Gurr shows that the audience would be likely to change considerably in type and number during the period 1567 to 1642. In order to determine a precise figure, it is necessary to take a 'snapshot' of the audience at a particular time. Harbage does so, and this paper has attempted to produce a similar snapshot from Cook's data. Gurr is particularly concerned with the evolution of the audience over time, and so a precise figure cannot readily be extrapolated from his analysis.

It will be clear how much of a process of supposition it is to try and estimate the size of the audience for Shakespeare's theatre. Any estimate of the percentage of the population who attended is reliant on other estimates, and it may be that any errors are simply compounded as one moves along. Depending on whose definition of the population of London is accepted, we arrive at a figure of between 9 per cent of London's population (Cook) and 13 per cent (Harbage) attending Shakespeare's theatre in 1605. What is certain from both estimates is that the great majority of Londoners did *not* attend Shakespeare's theatre.

Defining the size of the current audience for theatre in London is much simpler. Bearing in mind that the survey covered only the large London theatres, and not the small-scale fringe venues, an estimate of the percentage of the population of London who currently attend the theatre can be arrived at as follows. The parallel attendance survey to the audience survey monitored box-office receipts at all SWET member theatres every week. From the former type of survey, we know that during the period from 6 March 1990 to 5 March 1991, 11.3 million tickets were sold. The latter type, the audience survey, produced a result of 35 per cent of these tickets, or 4.0 million, being sold to residents of both the inner and outer London boroughs in the same period.

However, this figure of 4.0 million ticket sales does not mean that 4.0 million Londoners attended the theatre during that year. In this case, we do have information about the actual frequency of theatregoing by Londoners. Respondents in the survey were asked 'About how many visits have you made to theatres in London in the last 12 months, including this visit?' This should give a reasonable measure of the annual frequency of their theatregoing, barring any unusual events in recent months. From the City University's 1990-91 audience survey for SWET, based on 4360 replies from London borough residents, the annual frequency of theatregoing by Londoners can be broken down as follows:

One visit	8%
Two visits	10%
Three visits	11%
Four to six visits	26%
Seven to eleven visits	20%
Twelve to twenty visits	12%
Twenty-one to fifty visits	9%
More than fifty visits	4%

The survey was effectively a measure of the distribution of individual ticket sales, and not of ticket purchasers. This is because in theory the very frequent theatregoer stands a much greater chance of being encountered as part of the sample of theatregoers than the infrequent theatregoer does. To compensate for this, and to arrive at an estimate of the likely number of people buying these 4.0 million tickets, each ticket sale needs to be weighted by an amount inversely propor-

tional to the frequency of theatregoing of its purchaser. In simple terms, this means that because someone who attends the theatre on average three times a year is three times more likely to be sampled than someone who attends once a year, to arrive at an estimate of the number of people buying tickets, sales in the three visits a year category should be divided by three to find the correct number of ticket purchasers, and so on.

Yes, But Not So Often . . .

The usual convention when weighting categories that cover a range of frequencies is to take the mid-point of that category as the frequency to use in weighting. When weighting the highest frequency category, which simply says 'more than', the convention is usually to take the upper limit of that category as being twice the range of the previous category. In this case, the previous category had a range of 30 visits (21 to 50), so the limit of the upper category is taken to be 110, giving a range of 60 visits in the highest category.

If we weight all four million ticket purchases in this way, using the above data, we arrive at an estimate of approximately one million people living in the London boroughs going to the London theatre in the twelve-month survey period. The population of Greater London, as defined in the 1991 census, has been provisionally estimated at 6.378 million. This means that in the twelve month period from March 1990 to March 1991, around 16 per cent of the population of London attended the West End theatre.

Although this 16 per cent is very close to Harbage's estimate of 13 per cent of the population of London attending the theatre, the closeness of the two figures disguises some very major differences in theatregoing habits between 1605 and 1991. Both Harbage and Cook would place average weekly attendance in 1605 at around 21,000. While West End attendances vary considerably with the time of year, 230,000 in a week in 1991 would be not untypical, with around 80,000 of those tickets being sold to Londoners. So the number of Londoners going to the theatre in a particular week in 1991 is about four times as many as in 1605.

However, the population of London has increased by a factor of more than forty since 1605. If Londoners now went to the theatre as frequently as they did in 1605, we would have expected weekly attendances to have increased at least forty-fold since 1605, even with the percentage of the population who attend at all remaining the same.

To cater for the Jacobean level of interest in theatregoing among contemporary Londoners would require a massive theatre building programme, since current weekly West End capacity stands at around 355,000. As weekly attendances by Londoners since 1605 have increased only four-fold, while the population has increased more than forty-fold, we can conclude that the typical present-day Londoner who is a theatregoer goes to theatre in London only about once for every ten visits made by his Jacobean equivalent. While the typical Jacobean theatregoer may have gone to the theatre every week, the typical contemporary Londoner who goes to the theatre will go on average once every ten weeks.

The Arts Council commissions an annual survey on arts attendance from the British Market Research Bureau. Known as the Target Group Index, the survey includes information on what percentage of the population of Britain visits the theatre at all. The most recent results available, for 1989-90, show that 36 per cent of the population currently claim to attend theatre at all.[17] Although this relates to the whole of the UK, it is a much higher figure than the SWET results produced for the percentage of the London population who go to the theatre. The TGI figure falls to 24 per cent of the population when restricted to those who claim to attend plays, much closer to the SWET figure of 16 per cent. The apparent discrepancy between the SWET and TGI results suggests that much of what is claimed as current theatregoing by TGI interviewees is annual pantomime visits, or amateur and local theatregoing.

Present-day theatre is often spoken of as if it had a declining audience, as if it is not the mass appeal theatre of a previous golden age. Yet, while it is true that Londoners go to the theatre less often than in the Jacobean period, there is still a similar percentage of the local population displaying an interest in the London theatre as there apparently was in Shakespeare's time. An analysis of the three major texts on Shakespeare's audience suggests that theatre in London never was a theatre of truly mass appeal. The proliferation of leisure pursuits available to the present potential audience member may have made theatre in London a minority interest for the local population. But perhaps it always was.

Changes in Repertoire – and Seasons

Both Cook and Harbage have commented on the rapid turnover of plays in the Elizabethan and Jacobean period, with runs of just over a week being common. This is indicative of a small audience of frequent theatregoers who required a constant diet of new plays. In the present West End, the audience consists of many more people going far less frequently. This is one of the reasons why the West End is able to sustain long runs. *Cats*, by Andrew Lloyd Webber, has, for example, been running continuously for over twelve years at the time of writing. The West End theatre can draw on a constantly replenished pool of theatregoers, including many visitors to London, who only go and see a few shows a year.

Over the ten years during which the surveys have been carried out, the average age of the typical theatregoer has hardly changed. If the same people were going to the theatre in 1991 as were doing so in 1981, then the average age should have increased. This, and evidence from other surveys, suggests that certain ages and social circumstances tend to be closely associated with theatregoing, so that, for example, people go to the theatre far more often when they are in the 25-34 age bracket than they do once they reach their late thirties. If theatregoing is associated with social and domestic circumstances and changes in them, such as the arrival of children, then the theatre audience is constantly changing, even though its profile and numbers may be similar.

What we do not know is whether the long runs in the West End have come about in response to an audience of infrequent theatregoers whose theatregoing habits change with age, or whether the long runs have created this kind of audience, since their choice is obviously more limited when shows do not change very often. The importance of the tourist trade to London's theatres has been in part responsible for the success of long runs, but this mainly applies during the spring and summer months, and such shows continue to do very well during the autumn and winter.

The box-office returns research conducted in tandem with the SWET audience research allow some useful comparisons to be made with Harbage's analysis of popular plays and times of the year. Harbage finds that holidays tended to do better business than other times of year.[18] This is hardly surprising – holidays would mean that workers who could not normally go to the theatre would have a free day.

In the present West End, the situation is quite the opposite: holidays, especially bank holidays, tend to be the poorest periods of the year. This simply reflects the different leisure patterns then and now. Most theatre performances in the present day take place at times when most people are free to attend. At holiday periods, potential audiences tend to leave London. The holiday frees them to follow other competing leisure pursuits, in the same way as it freed the Elizabethan working man to attend the theatre.

Harbage also notes that new plays tended to do better business than old ones, and that an average run consisted of about twelve performances.[19] So few performances suggests a rapid exhaustion of the potential audience, and tends to confirm the theory that the actual number of theatregoers, as opposed to theatre entrance fees paid, was very small.

In the present West End, where the audience is drawn from a much wider pool, and where performance times do not limit the potential audience in the same way as they did with the Elizabethan and Jacobean theatre, new plays tend to be less successful than revivals and large-scale musicals. For example, productions of modern drama in the West End in 1991 achieved on average 57 per cent of capacity, while modern musicals sold 76 per cent.

The Elizabethan and Jacobean audience may have been primarily attracted by novelty. Audience surveys suggest that the present-day London audience is largely, though not exclusively, attracted by the familiar and the safe. When musical audiences are asked about the reason they have chosen to attend, their reply is often linked to factors such as the reassurance of knowing that there is something they will enjoy, because they may know one or more of the songs. Andrew Lloyd Webber's name in particular is sufficiently well-known to act as an expected guarantee of enjoyment for many people. With the average ticket price in the West End currently topping £20, and many theatregoers making only one or two visits a year to the theatre in order to celebrate a special occasion such as a birthday or anniversary, some kind of guarantee of enjoyment is clearly important.

Analysis of the Audience

Analysis of the demographic profile of Shakespeare's audience relies on making certain assumptions about the likely effects of social conditions. These conditions in turn may have to be deduced from contemporary documents – raising the related problem of the reliability of the evidence. Some of the circumstances affecting the likely profile of Shakespeare's theatregoers are readily apparent – for example, the effects of available transport to and distance from the theatres. In Shakespeare's time, the great majority of the audience would have been London residents, either permanently or for the season. Harbage notes, for example, that attendances were good during the legal terms[20] – simply because easy access to the theatre would have been a major determinant of attendance.

In the present day, Londoners account for only around 35 per cent of all ticket sales, and overseas visitors form an important sector of the current West End audience – 32 per cent in the most recent SWET survey. While there was certainly the occasional overseas visitor to Shakespeare's theatre, and indeed one of the most famous of contemporary sketches of Elizabethan theatre was made by an overseas visitor to London,[21] the logistics of travel to the theatre in Shakespeare's time would have excluded people who lived outside London, unless they were visiting London for several days for other reasons.

Cook notes that London 'seasons' were popular among country gentlemen, and it seems likely that such theatregoers formed an important part of Shakespeare's audience at appropriate times of year. Day trippers, and others making short visits to London remain a vital part of the West End audience. In the 1990-91 audience surveys, 37 per cent of all those theatregoers who were not London residents had come to the capital on a day trip.

Access to the theatres by various forms of transport thus remains an important determinant of audience profile. Towns from outside London which are important sources of present-day London theatregoers are almost without exception on major British Rail lines. Oxford, Watford, Reading, St. Albans, and Cambridge consistently feature as important sources of theatregoers. Improvements in speed and method of travel to the theatre since Elizabethan and Jacobean times may have resulted in the audience being drawn from a wider geographical area than previously, but it is still that area which is within a few hours travelling distance which accounts for the majority of theatregoers. Although perceived as being of major importance to the present-day London theatre, overseas visitors have not yet outnumbered local residents in any of the surveys so far conducted across the whole West End.

The Matter of Class

Much contemporary Elizabethan comment displays concern over the number of 'lower-class' people who may be encountered at the theatre:

the quality of such as frequent the sayed playes, beeing the ordinary places of meeting for all vagrant persons and maisterles men that hang about the Citie, theeves, horsestealers, whoremongers, coozeners, connycatching persones, practizers of treason, and other such lyke.[22]

The writers of such diatribes are often public officials, using the supposed contaminating effect of such groups, and their potential for riot and affray, in petitions against the theatres when seeking restrictions and closures. Arts managers in the present day tend to be more concerned at the negative effects of audiences supposedly being restricted to the upper and middle classes, and in the case of subsidized venues there is often felt to be a responsibility to comply with the directives about widening access in the Arts Council Charter. In purely commercial theatre ventures, the concern centres around the restricted size of the audience when it is drawn from only one sector of society.

Cook argues against the partial view of the railers against the Elizabethan theatre. Having established that the privileged in London society would have been sufficient in number to sustain Shakespeare's theatre, without the need to draw on large numbers of the working classes, she argues the case for the majority of Shakespeare's audience being of necessity from the privileged on several grounds – for example, that only they would have available leisure time during the afternoon, the usual performance time.

The evening performance times of the present day do not place major restrictions on the number of people who can attend the London theatre, although in the surveys there are usually some theatregoers from the London suburbs who complain that 7.30 pm starts make it difficult for them to get to the theatre on time. Matinees in the West End, not surprisingly, tend to attract a specialized audience of older, retired people, tourists and organized groups.

The widespread availability of leisure during typical performance times will not necessarily result in a wide social spread of the audience in the present day. Although the SWET survey does not collect data on social class, the TGI survey suggests that the higher the social class, the more likely people are to go to the theatre. No fewer than 60 per cent of the AB class in the most recent TGI survey class thus claimed to 'currently attend' the theatre: this falls to 19 per cent of the DE class.[23]

These results relate to the whole of the UK. AB social classes account for 26 per cent of all theatregoers, even though they account for only 16 per cent of the UK population. However, because those in the DE social class form a much larger percentage of the UK population than the ABs (31 per cent are DEs, compared with 16 per cent ABs),[24] they form an important section of the theatre audience, even though a much smaller percentage of them attend the theatre. Fifteen per cent of all theatregoers in the TGI survey were from social class DE.

According to Cook, the 'privileged' in Shakespeare's time accounted for around 15 per cent of the population of London, but for the great majority of attendances.[25] Even if we accept Gurr's assertion that Cook's analysis of the social composition of the audience may be somewhat narrower than the reality, it is still apparently the case that the social spread of the audience is now much greater than it was in Shakespeare's time. The greater availability of leisure time and the changes in performance times which followed the advent of artificial lighting have made this wider social spread possible.

Comparative Costs of Theatregoing

Costs are another factor which Cook argues could dictate audience profile. She notes that a clothworker's annual wage was £5 in 1589,[26] equivalent to 23 pence per week. Admission to the public playhouses at that time could be had for one penny.[27] In theory, therefore, a clothworker would have to expend only 4 per cent of his weekly income to visit Shakespeare's theatre.

Drawing comparisons between the spending power of a worker in Elizabethan times and in the present day is complicated by several factors. Tax systems differ greatly, while items such as food cost much more in real terms in Elizabethan times and so money available for leisure spending might be less. Renumeration in Elizabethan times often included extras such as board and lodging. According to Cook, however, 'it would be a mistake to assume that low prices meant a low clientele. Many a man of unquestioned privilege had very little ready money.'[28]

Cook takes the availability of low prices to reflect the desire of theatre managers to attract the impoverished gentleman rather than to make theatre available to a wide range of classes. She writes in support of her main thesis that Shakespeare's audience was drawn largely from the privileged classes. What is clear, however, is that admission to the playhouse was in theory within the financial reach of 'low clientele', whether or not other circumstances permitted them to attend.

In the present day, a rough comparison of the accessibility of London theatres related to price may be attempted. The cheapest ticket available in the West End theatres in July 1992 was £3. The average weekly wage of a manual worker at March 1992 was £275.65.[29] The manual worker in the present day would thus have to expend only one per cent of his gross income to buy a West End theatre ticket. Even the purchase of a £20 ticket, the current West End average price, would require only seven per cent of his weekly gross income.

However, the issue of how far price affects theatre attendance, and of how strong a relationship there is between social class and a willingness and ability to pay ticket prices, is less clear cut than a comparison of wages with prices might suggest. A recent study by Peter Walshe of Millward Brown for the Arts Council and the Scottish Arts Council[30] showed that price was fairly low down in the factors affecting arts attendances. Thus, out of 1,298 people questioned, only 19 people (1.5 per cent) mentioned price.

In assessing the factors influencing their theatregoing, even young, unemployed, C2DE, or infrequent attenders put price below quality and subject matter or story. The overall message of the Millward Brown survey was that when people wished to attend, price in itself did not figure greatly as a deterrent. The relative lack of young people among present-day theatre audiences is often regretted (in the most recent SWET survey, 11 per cent of all tickets were sold to those in full-time education), and attributed to high prices. But a typical price for a pop concert at Wembley is £25, well above the current average West End price of just under £20. When audiences want to see something, price in itself is not a strong determinant of their likelihood to attend.

It may be that to draw conclusions about the nature of Shakespeare's audience on the basis of price is unrealistic, since the available prices would have permitted a wide variety of income groups to attend, without necessarily making a theatre visit a desirable activity for them. Simply, reliable data on exactly what kind of people constituted the audience for Shakespeare's theatre is not available, and has to be deduced from related evidence.

Shakespeare's Plays in London

The current audience surveys for SWET do give a representative picture of the present London theatre audience. While it is not possible to compare audience profiles in the two periods, it is possible to compare the audience for Shakespeare now with the audience for other plays in London, and to examine what effect the status of Shakespeare as part of the cultural heritage might have had on audience profile.

The Shakespeare plays which have been surveyed as part of the SWET audience surveys are *All's Well That Ends Well*, *A Midsummer Night's Dream*, *Richard II*, and *Richard III*. The choice of plays to survey was dictated by what happened to be in the repertoire at the time of the surveys. The following are fairly broad generalizations, based on an analysis of around 30,000 theatregoers over a ten-year period. The results for Shakespeare audiences have been quite consistent throughout this period. However, it should be remembered that the following refers only to the audience for Shakespeare in London. It is probable that audiences for Shakespeare in Stratford upon Avon, and in other theatres outside London, would have a different profile.

The most important audience for Shakespeare in the present day is drawn from the London boroughs. However, compared with other productions in the subsidized sector, such as opera and dance, Shakespeare productions attract a larger overseas audience. This may be because Shakespeare has a position as part of the British cultural heritage in a way that opera and dance do not.

Audiences for Shakespeare are very regular theatregoers – far more so than audiences for other types of play. Once-a-month theatre visits are not unusual among the present day audience for Shakespeare, although this does not seem very frequent when compared with the once-a-week which is thought to be typical of the theatre audience in Shakespeare's time. What we do not know is whether the once-monthly theatre visits of the present-day audience for Shakespeare are confined to Shakespeare and other classical drama, or whether they range across different types of show.

The converse of this frequent theatregoing is that Shakespeare at present attracts very few newcomers to theatre. Thus, even students and young people who do attend Shakespeare tend to go to other productions during the year. But young people do form an important part of the audience for Shakespeare. Compared with other types of production in the mainly subsidized sector, Shakespeare attracts more young people than opera – but fewer than dance.

Women predominate among the audience for Shakespeare, more so than for most commercial productions in London. A high percentage of the audience for Shakespeare makes a special visit to London to come to the theatre. This includes overseas visitors to Shakespeare, who are typically more likely to have come to Britain on a theatregoing trip than to have come primarily for a sight-seeing holiday.

Large groups form a vital part of the audience for Shakespeare – not simply school and student parties, but work outings, and organized club visits. This is one thing that has changed in recent years, with the group audience for Shakespeare increasing in importance since the mid-1980s.

Shakespeare's name was consistently the most important reason for people choosing to attend a production of Shakespeare, and they were far less influenced by reviews than audiences for modern drama or for comedy. However, Shakespeare productions were one of the few categories in which the director's name was likely to be an influence in the choice of which production to see.

The audience for Shakespeare is highly educated. In the 1990-91 surveys, over half of all those surveyed at a performance of Shakespeare had been educated to at least university or college level. Existing students also formed a very important part of the audience. However unfortunate such associations may be, it is likely that Shakespeare is for many people associated with theatre as education. This perception may be the most important determinant of Shakespeare's audience in the present day, rather than the accessibility or otherwise of the theatres themselves.

In theory at least, if we look at prices, performance times, and transport access to the theatres, the London theatre of the present day is accessible to a much wider range of social classes than was the case in Elizabethan and Jacobean times. However, the evidence suggests that theatregoing behaviour has changed considerably since the sixteenth and seventeenth centuries. Approximately the same percentage of the population of London seems to go to the theatre now as in Shakespeare's time. However, people are attending much less frequently, and the much slower turnover of repertoire when compared with Shakespeare's time may be either cause or effect of the lower frequency of London theatregoing.

Notes and References

1. P. H. Mann, 'Surveying a Theatre Audience: Methodological Problems', *British Journal of Sociology*, XVII, No. 4 (December 1966).

2. National Opinion Polls, *Theatregoing in London*, unpublished survey conducted for the Society of West End Theatre, April 1981.

3. Ibid.

4. Alfred Harbage, *Shakespeare's Audience* (New York, 1941); Ann Jennalie Cook, *The Privileged Playgoers of Shakespeare's London 1576-1642* (Princeton, 1981); Andrew Gurr, *Playgoing in Shakespeare's London* (Cambridge, 1987).

5. Gurr, p. 4

6. Bernard Levin, 'The Sickness at the Heart of London's Theatre', *Sunday Times*, 29 January 1978.

7. This figure is derived from the parallel study to that conducted for SWET, conducted by Michael Quine of City University for the TMA (Theatrical Management Association), whose membership covers virtually all but the smallest fringe theatres and companies outside London. Both the TMA and SWET studies include commercial and subsidized theatres and companies, though there are far fewer of the latter in the West End.

8. Gurr, p. 85.

9. Charles M. Clode, *Memorials of the Guild of Merchant Taylors*, Vol. I (1875), p 578, quoted in Harbage, p. 13.

10. Harbage, p. 41.

11. Cook, p. 17.

12. Cook, p. 192.

13. Cook, p. 193.

14. Most notably, she makes use of figures from A. L. Rowse, *The England of Elizabeth* (London, 1950), and Peter Ramsey, *Tudor Economic Problems* (London, 1963).

15. Cook, p. 179.

16. Gurr, p. 3

17. *Target Group Index 1989-90*, conducted by BRMB for the Arts Council of Great Britain (ACGB, 1990).

18. Harbage, p. 46.

19. Harbage, p. 43.

20. Harbage, p. 176-7.

21. The Johannes De Witt sketch of the Swan playhouse from 1596, in a drawing by Arendt van Buchel, is reproduced in most illustrated theatre histories of the period, and can be found in Gurr, p. 17.

22. Lord Mayor to Lord Burghley, 3 November 1594, quoted in Gurr, p. 210.

23. *Target Group Index*, op. cit.

24. The source is the JICNARS national readership survey, June 1990, reproduced in Advertising Association, *Marketing Pocket Book 1991* (London, 1991).

25. Cook, p. 94.

26. Cook, p. 279.

27. Cook, p. 181.

28. Cook, p. 182.

29. HMSO, *Employment Gazette*, June 1992.

30. Peter Walshe, 'What Price the Live Arts?', summarized in *The Insider*, Arts Council, No 10 (Spring 1991), p. 7.

NTQ Reports and Announcements

Maggie Gale

The Magdalena 'Raw Visions' Project

SINCE the first Magdalena Project in 1986, (reported in NTQ11) as many as thirty events have been mounted by this 'International Network of Women in Contemporary Theatre'. The purpose of 'Raw Visions – Strategies for Survival 1993', held at Chapter Arts Centre in Cardiff from 1 to 3 July, was to encourage the work of younger women theatre practitioners by providing them with advice from experienced professional performers, directors, and dramaturgs, as well as administrators, and representatives of funding bodies.

Previous Magdalena festivals have used either the short intensive workshop formula, where leaders work with ten or more participants over a number of days, or, as in the 'V Lines' project (1991), provided an environment for practitioners to make work with participants over a period of weeks. For 'Raw Visions', ten young practitioners were invited to bring projects in progress on which they could work with invited leaders in the mornings. The seventy or so other participants spent the mornings either in group and one-to-one consultations, or in 'swop shop' sessions where information, ideas, and advice could be shared in an informal structure. During the afternoons and evenings there were talks and work demonstrations, or presentations given by women working in all areas of theatre. The festival opened with a performance of *Nakasone* by Brigitte Cirla, of Voix Polyphonique, France, and ended with Julia Varley of Odin Teatret in *The Castle of Holstebro*.

Making and Marketing Work The point made by Gilly Adams, who is on the Management Board of Magdalena and was formerly a Drama Officer of the Welsh Arts Council, that it is vital, in a time of economic recession, for women artists to find ways of surviving whereby they can maintain their integrity and retain control over their work while still getting it seen, proved to be a predominant theme of the three days. One of the most important elements of the festival was thus the discourse on economic strategies for survival.

The women talking from the point of view of administrative and managerial experience stressed the necessity for younger companies and performers to abide by a number of factors when making work, trying to sell it, or simply getting it seen. Both Jill Greenhalgh (Artistic Director, Magdalena) and Gilly Adams stressed the importance of:

• knowing exactly what you want, who you want to work with, and who the work is being made for;
• going to see as much theatre and performance work as possible and seeing what other practitioners are doing;
• investigating the variety of ways in which different people work, and learning from the working processes of others as a way of learning about your own;
• not feeling as if the 'victim' role is the only one for women: realizing that funding structures are accessible, that 'techno-fear' is not enough of a justification for thinking that funding applications can only be filled out by funders.

These ideas were backed up later by Alexandra Ankrah (Arts Council Women in Art Project) in her talk 'Patronage and Patriarchy – an Almost Practical Guide to the Arts Funding Structure'. Alexandra was very clear about the importance of finding out how funding structures work, what your potential position is within the structures, and how to find ways round the rigidity of arts funding bureaucracy and bias.

Economic Strategies Alongside Lois Keiden, Jill Greenhalgh, while chairing the group consultation session on Economic Strategies, talked about the necessity to make work regardless of the availability of funding. What came out of the session when thrown open into a brainstorming forum was that it was as important now as it was twenty years ago not to be confined by the availability of 'traditional' theatre venues. Many of the participants were showing their work in community centres, village or church halls, and even (in the case of one Birmingham group) in shop windows. Jill Greenhalgh cited the case of Bobby Baker, whose earlier work was performed in kitchens.

The word 'networking' was recurrent, and both Jill and earlier Geddy Aniksdal (Grenland Friteatre, Norway), in her talk 'It's Hopeless and We Won't Give Up', discussed the possibility and experience of international touring based on 'swop hosting'. Both women stressed the importance of being bureaucratically organized as a means of attaining artistic freedom: as Geddy put it, it's okay to be a 'petit bourgeois bureaucrat if it means that you can be an artistic anarchist'.

Networking The integration of artists, administrators, and consultants made the seemingly impossible into a working possibility. The working relationships and friendships which have grown amongst the founders of and participants in the Magdalena Project over the last ten years were living proof that it is vital to network and, as both Jill and Lois stated on more than one occasion, to 'make friends' and use performance forums, such as the National Review of Live Art, as a way of doing this as well as getting your own work seen and seeing that of others.

Jill also wanted women to recognize alternative possibilities of funding, the importance of approaching the right people with the right information, of integrating one's work with the community in which it is being made, reaching out to all audiences, setting up co-productions, and so on. The emphasis was on using all available resources, and making use of ITC courses and of workshops with international practitioners, such as those organized by International Workshop Festival, Physical State International, and the Centre for Performance Research.

Selling Your Work   All the administrators from their different professional perspectives considered 'straight videos' more appropriate to the 1990s than the glossy publicity and 'pop videos' which many theatre companies were coerced into using for their marketing strategies in the 1980s. The collective experience of the Magdalena women has shown that work must come before funding, that it is as important to develop an administrative structure and working process which is relevant to the performance or theatre work being produced as it is to sell it.

Consultation and Private Sessions   The purpose of these sessions was to give individual women an opportunity to seek advice from the leaders in their varying capacities as professional theatre workers. During a number of the sessions many of the points raised in the lectures were reiterated, but rather than finding this disappointing the women I talked to declared the openness and frankness refreshing, informative, and encouraging.

Many of the sessions ended up affirming ideas which younger performers had previously felt to be invalidated, giving suggestions for possible future pathways, or simply providing encouragement and a listening ear for the 'next' generation who have begun their working lives in the economic aftermath of the 1980s. These sessions served to narrow the gap between the experiences of the invited leaders and the aspirations of the festival participants.

For one consultation session, Pilar Gutierre, a Spanish performer based in Wales, was working on an adaptation for performance of a Tennessee Williams short story with Brigitte Kaquet (from Cirques Divers, Belgium). Brigitte helped her to 'play' with the information and research which

she had gathered, illuminating possible clues for approaches to blocking the narratives, recommending relevant books, ideas, images, and so on. She asked Pilar to identify objects from her research which could be worked with physically, encouraging her to find surprises and different energy levels within the text, and helped her to pare down the research into elements which would be useful for the making of a performance.

As an example of one of the private sessions, Sue Richardson, whose work has been shown in Wales, Canada, and London, worked with Susan Bassnett (writer and university teacher, England) on her research for a new piece based on the relationship between women and travel. Susan suggested ways of fixing and opening up the text, and finding ways of using theatrical space which were intimated by the themes of the research and subject-matter of the performance.

Kathy Haines (Posh Frocks, Devon) worked with Sylvia Riccardelli (Koreja, Italy) during the morning sessions of the festival on ideas concerning the editing of performance material, putting the transitional moments from daily life into theatrical life, and paring down and defining theatrical moments alongside the comparative application of 'everyday' training and points of view or experience.

Most of the women who took part in the private sessions found the work both inspiring and generous on the part of the leaders, who integrated their experiences as performers and teachers in a way which far exceeded the expectations of those with whom they were working.

Lectures and Work Demonstrations   A number of the invited practitioners chose the lecture format for exposing the intricacies of their working processes. Chris Fry, for example, gave a detailed and insightful paper on the history and development of the Magdalena Project on the first day of the festival. Susan Bassnett, in 'Biography/ Autobiography', talked about the way in which much of her current work stems from an interest in the borders and frontiers between writers, academia, theatre, historical periods, geography, and generations. For her there is an inextricable link between fact and fiction, as there is between the life of the writer and that about which the writer writes. Her basic analysis of the impetus for auto/biographical writing and research aligned the process with that of the making of theatre, including elements such as the mixing of 'times', voyeurism, exposure, looking for different 'truths', and so on.

The interweaving of the personal and the empirical was also an integral component of Brigitte Kaquet's 'One View of Dramaturgy and Direction'. Presented on the last day of the festival, Brigitte's paper provided an extraordinary and rare insight into the processes involved in the

88

construction and interweaving of theatrical narratives. This was one of the most revealing and intellectually stimulating papers of the festival – the construction of the paper itself, an indicator of the pathways taken in the processes of researching the dramaturgical creation.

Julia Varley ('The Dead Brother'), Tanith Noble ('How to Set, Frame, and Direct Theatrical Improvisations'), and Brigitte Cirla ('Music in Theatre') gave formal presentations which showed their respective working methods as they have developed during their careers as performers and directors, while Teresa Ralli (Yuyachkani, Peru) and Geddy Aniksdal gave work demonstrations in which they shared elements of their training methods and working processes with a delighted audience who fully appreciated the precision and discipline involved.

Silvia Riccardelli's 'Outliving – a Way In and Out of the Theatre' was an extremely moving and witty presentation based on her work and training as an actress, and on a questioning of what she can now teach younger women through her theatre experience. Through her autobiographical performance structure and content she questioned the balance of loss and gain when working in theatre, concluding that it was a continuous experience fed by the interaction between theatre and the outside world.

One of the most significant aspects of the work discussed was the fact that it had grown out of years of working collaboratively in small groups all over the world. Many of these groups have had to find ways of surviving through adapting to the needs of their communities and to changes in the economic climate. Training and performing have existed alongside the development of creating and adapting working environments, making links and networks with other small theatre companies, teaching, and so on. Geddy Aniksdal's statement of the need 'for artists to have more than one leg to stand on' if they want to survive was at once a warning and an encouragement for the younger generation of practitioners at the festival.

The performance on the last day of Sandra Pasini and Antonella Diana's *Colour Your Heart* was perhaps a sign of new directions for future Magdalena festivals. Having worked on and off over the last few years with Julia Varley, they had paid their own expenses in order to bring their work from Italy to Cardiff, insisting that it be shown at the festival.

During the plenary session, it became clear that as well as wanting to maintain the intensive workshop structure, the 'new generation' of Magdalena women wanted to be able to show and discuss their own work as well as have regular repetitions of the 'Raw Visions' working structure. Plans are currently being made to create an international festival in September 1994 with a multi-tiered structure, intended to bring together workshops, demonstrations, and performance by both experienced practitioners and the new generation of performers.

The 'Raw Visions' festival was a landmark in terms of the way in which it prioritized the accessing of information and validated women's experiences and hopes. All of the invited practitioners were in constant demand, and extra sessions eagerly sought in any available gap. In a theatre world where it becomes more and more difficult to gain funding or even the possibilities for live performance, those who have been with Magdalena since its inception and those whose work has grown through their involvement in the project made themselves open to questions and shared their mistakes and experiences.

As a result, the festival demystified many of the processes involved in making and showing theatre for women who had just finished training or were in the early stages of their theatre careers, and provided a valuable working link between different generations of women theatre practitioners. A fundamental aim of the Magdalena Project is to 'create an artistic environment and economic structure which enables women to work and for their work to be taken seriously': the 'Raw Visions' festival was living proof that this continues to be achieved.

Information on past and future Magdalena Project events, and on the Magdalena 1994 Festival, can be obtained from The Magdalena Project, Chapter, Market Road, Canton, Cardiff CF5 1QE, Wales (telephone and fax 0222-220552).

Glenn Loney

Gay Plays, Straight Plays

GONE ARE THE DAYS when Broadway producers were terrified of dealing with 'difficult' sexuality on stage, not to mention explicit sexual behaviour. Where *Oh! Calcutta!* celebrated heterosexual pleasures, however, now a number of new plays and musicals centre on homosexual characters, their problems and occasional epiphanies – quite a change from the days when *The Green Bay Tree* or *Trio*, hinting darkly at same-sex attractions, shocked some, and left many in their audiences baffled, since such relationships were completely outside their experience. Or so they thought.

Today, thanks to all kinds of exposure on television, but notably because of the continuing tragedy of Aids, 'the love that dare not speak its name' has become almost a household word. Yet as the visibility of the gay life-style has increased, so have naked prejudices and overt acts of violence: and neither the more confrontational demonstrations of 'Act Up' nor the dubious sport of 'outing' closeted celebrities – supposedly to reveal them as role-models, though the effect more often has been to humiliate and damage them in the public eye – have won embattled gays the acceptance they sought.

In the theatre, too, there may be a danger that the current emphasis on gays and their hopes and dreams may be alienating a predominantly heterosexual audience. John Simon is hardly the only drama critic to have taken Tennessee Williams and other gay playwrights to task for veiling their interests and experiences with hetero-gauze, and in the new climate of theatrical freedom Williams would surely have written frankly and powerfully, were he with us: but Blanche du Bois remains a vivid *female* portrait – she's not Williams in drag, as some tart-tongued reviewers have surmised. Like Flaubert and Mme. Bovary, Blanche was thoroughly known to Williams.

Years ago, the Kinsey Report speculated that a tenth of the population might have had some homosexual experience. A dubious recent survey yielded a figure nearer one per cent – surely from a skewed sample? If that really were correct, how could one account for such a plenitude of gay dramas, comedies, and musicals during the past season? Producers and those in the commercial sector must fill seats, make money, and hope for extended runs, and even not-for-profit institutional theatres cannot afford to offend wealthy donors or too many single-seat subscribers. Apparently gay issues no longer worry them.

This is a good sign. But isn't it a bit much to go to the theatre (as critics in New York often do) eight times in one week, only to discover that every production has in some way, peripherally or centrally, dealt with homosexuality? True, there was only *one* week when that happened – but it would have been unthinkable before the onset of the Aids crisis. It is of course a double irony that it has taken a national disaster like Aids to lead so many heterosexual Americans – often families and friends of Aids victims – to discard previous aversions or prejudices about gay citizens. It is therefore all to the good that the theatre has become an important and vivid forum for discussing gay problems – which is certainly not the case so far with film.

At the same time, it would also be welcome to have some powerful new straight plays about 'straight' Americans. The country is in a social, economic, political, and cultural crisis, something for which gays can hardly be blamed. But where are the new Arthur Millers to deal with these themes? This past season, several gay playwrights did in fact write 'straight' straight plays, but with mixed results. Can it be that most of the straight playwrights have gone to Hollywood? The financial rewards are certainly better.

At the close of the season in New York, two major gay productions premiered shortly before the Tony nominations, eclipsing memories of fall openings. (This strategy resembles the practice of releasing films just before Oscar-time.) These two 'blockbusters' – *Angels in America* and *Kiss of the Spider Woman* – were, oddly enough, both first seen in London, which now seems to have replaced Boston as a tryout town for Broadway.

Tony Kushner's *Angels*, subtitled 'A Gay Fantasy on National Themes', was represented initially by the first of its two parts, *Millennium Approaches*. Focusing on a gay couple, one of whom is dying of Aids, and a married Mormon couple – the husband tormented by gay longings – *Angels* explores American fictions and realities with an often slashing wit and a wild sense of the surreal. Having a bright-winged angel crash through the ceiling at the close is not only a *coup de théâtre*, but a vividly surreal metaphor. There have been native playwrights who have dabbled in the strange and the whimsical – none more charmingly than John Guare – but Kushner seems the first to have dared such astonishments in the service of deeply serious problems concerning individuals in a chaotic society.

Ron Leibman gives a bravura performance as the closeted homophobe, Roy Cohn. The real Cohn was far more reserved and serpentine, and this is in fact the basic hyperactive Leibman *shtik*, but it galvanizes the audience. In Robin Wagner's ingenious settings, director George C. Wolfe – new chief of Joe Papp's Public Theatre – has helped the cast generate an unremitting energy and a driving pace.

Many reviewers noted that the show was so taut one didn't notice the passage of its three and a half hours playing time. In fact, *Angels* would have more impact with deft cutting. An incident of night-time buggery in a park provides a cue for outraged patrons to leave mid-drama: clearly, the shock has a point, but some spectators aren't ready for it. Perhaps they would prefer in the theatre the curious compromise offered gays in the military: 'Don't ask, don't tell.'

Hal Prince's impressive and fast-moving production of *Kiss of the Spiderwoman* profits from its workshop-style staging at SUNY-Purchase and later experiences in Toronto and London. Brent Carver, as the lonely gay window-dresser Molina, was remarkable: touching, irritating, and ultimately transcendent. And Chita Rivera, as the movie star whose films and persona obsess the

Ellen McLaughlin as the Angel and Stephen Spinella as Prior Walter in *Millennium Approaches*, the first part of Tony Kushner's *Angels in America*, at the Walter Kerr Theatre. Photo: Joan Marcus.

imprisoned Molina, was dazzling, though the ingenious choreography was designed to make her dancing seem even more spectacular than it was.

Manuel Puig's fiction suggests that Molina eventually wins the love of the tough revolutionary who shares his cell. In the musical, the cell-mate uses sex to get Molina to pass a dangerous message when he's released. Prince again deploys seeming tons of metal bars in this Jerome Sirlin set – recalling Prince's scaffoldings in *Sweeney Todd* and other musicals. Something more in the vein of the magic realism of Puig's story might have been even more magical. Sirlin's overlaid projections didn't achieve that, nor did John Kander and Fred Ebb's songs have the instant dramatic impact of their *Cabaret* score: but greater familiarity may breed fondness for them.

Falsettos, an award-winning musical dealing with Aids, was a popular Broadway hold-over from last season. The other musical survivals didn't even hint at homosexuality: *Cats, Crazy for You, Guys and Dolls, Jelly's Last Jam, Les Mis, Miss Saigon, Phantom,* and *Will Rogers' Follies* – though Rogers was famous for commenting, 'I never met a man I didn't like!'

New and more astonishing than *Spiderwoman*, at least in production values, was the Who's *Tommy*, reworked from its earlier concert and film versions by its creator, Pete Townshend, and its dynamic director, Des McAnuff, who brought it to Broadway from California's La Jolla Playhouse, where McAnuff is artistic director. Critics were quick to note that the autistic young Tommy was sexually abused by his wicked old Uncle Ernie, thus enabling them to include the musical in the gay census.

With the brilliant choreography of Wayne Cilento and the frantic pace set by McAnuff, this show – also driven by the pounding beat of Townshend's score – is an overwhelming audio-visual experience. Designers John Arnone, David Woolard, Chris Parry, and Wendall Harrington have achieved the explosive, constantly changing impact of Music-TV, but in three dimensions, not two – some of the colourful projections recalling the images of Gilbert and George. Only when one is back home, recovering from the frenzy, does one realize how utterly simple the fable is, and how flat and pat its ending: after epic triumphs as a pinball master, Tommy returns home to his parents and Uncle Ernie.

Gayness is not central to Wendy Wasserstein's *The Sisters Rosensweig*, but one of her Three Sisters is engaged to a bisexual who finally abandons her for a man – a British director, very witty, played by John Vickery. But Robert Klein, as a mature fake-furrier from New York who flutters the seemingly cold heart of Britified Brooklynite Sara Goode (Jane Alexander), is warmly wry and amusing.

Wasserstein says she thought she was being Chekhovian, but her trio of Jewish siblings – each quite different – gets gales of laughter from audiences in ways Olga, Irena, and Masha never could. Madeline Kahn plays to perfection a sexually frustrated, religion-obsessed, modish suburban housewife she describes offstage as 'The Yenta from Hell'. Dan Sullivan staged this Broadway hit for another institutional theatre, not in California but in Manhattan: the Lincoln Center Theatre. Sullivan is himself artistic director of the Seattle Repertory.

In the current climate, reviewers perforce detected in Lynn Redgrave's delightful one-woman show, *Shakespeare for My Father*, allusions to Sir Michael Redgrave's 'bisexuality'. One hardly noticed, so vibrant was her performance, interweaving Shakespearean scenes and quotes with memories of her growing up as a Redgrave and an actress. The quotes were cues for spurring her narrative along, always trying to win approval – or even mere notice – from her often indifferent father.

Gay characters, problems, and themes were more in evidence away from Broadway, partly because audiences are more adventurous but also because the producing theatres are often institutional not-for-profit operations, supported by grants, patrons, and subscribers. Paul Rudnick's *Jeffrey*, initially staged by the WPA Theatre, almost instantly became a comedy hit, soon moving to an off-Broadway commercial venue. The author of *I Hate Hamlet* followed that farce with something almost incredible: an Aids play that is satirical, witty, bumptious – and often farcical.

After such angry manifestos as *The Normal Heart* and *As Is*, Aids seemed the decade's most tragic domestic topic: but Rudnick suggests that, even under a seeming death sentence, life is still worth living as fully as possible. Jeffrey (John Michael Higgins) is a waiter/actor, desperately celibate to avoid Aids, but fated to fall in love with a handsome HIV-positive male. Rudnick doesn't ignore Aids fatalities: he puts them in focus, easing the pain, and his deftly affectionate mocking of the fantasies, hopes, fetishes, and pretensions of New York's gay scene seemed to delight both gay and straight spectators.

Paula Vogel's *Baltimore Waltz*, shown last season by Circle Rep and now being widely produced at home and abroad, had many wryly comic moments: and it, too, was about an Aids death. This season she dug into her trunk to give Circle Rep an earlier play, *And Baby Makes Seven*, in which Aids was not an issue, but the problem was of two lesbian lovers trying to conceive a child without artificial insemination. This they did by inspiring their gay room-mate with male images to bring him to climax.

Vogel imagined the couple as having three *imaginary* children – whose voices the two

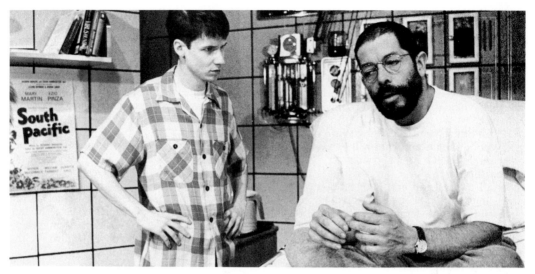

John Cameron Mitchell and Jonathan Hardy in the Circle Repertory production of *The Destiny of Me*, Larry Kramer's sequel to *The Normal Heart*. Photo: Martha Swope Associates.

women coyly interpreted – who do not welcome the idea of a real child in the picturesque loft designed by Derek McLane. At least in Albee's *Who's Afraid of Virginia Woolf?* the imaginary child never spoke! Vogel teaches playwriting at Brown University, so she may have clones in the works.

Barbara Graham's *Camp Paradox*, set in 1963 at a girls' summer camp, explored varieties of teenage silliness and sexual longing, culminating in a brief and painful liaison between a sensitive, confused camper and a devout Roman Catholic counsellor who has fairly rigid notions of how she and her young lover will live together. This was handsomely produced by the WPA – perhaps as a balance to *Jeffrey*?

David Drake's one-man show, *The Night Larry Kramer Kissed Me*, was a brilliant, furious series of set pieces on the challenges of growing up gay in America, athletically performed by the author with rapid-fire changes of mood and pace. Its title refers to the author of *The Normal Heart*, the first real Aids drama to denounce the initial indifference of the establishment and the media to this deadly disease. This season, Kramer himself returned to the fray with the semi-autobiographical *The Destiny of Me* – another Circle Rep production – with Jonathan Hadary as Ned Weeks, an Aids victim in a government facility rather like the Walter Reed Hospital outside Washington, D. C.

Weeks's cohorts, like Kramer's, have massed outside to protest the government's seeming failure to find a cure for Aids, even while Week's doctor – very like the Surgeon General – is in fact doing all he can to save or extend his angry patient's life. And there are flashbacks of family life to explain the pain of growing up gay in a hostile atmosphere. The play had a certain angry power but did not last the season.

At the tiny Kampo Cultural and Multimedia Center in the East Village, two studiously serious plays by Lee Blessing centred on gay problems: *Patient A* and *Lake Street Extension*. Blessing was in fact commissioned by the family of Kimberly Bergalis to tell her story. Infected with Aids by her HIV-positive dentist, the understandably angry virgin Bergalis died painfully of the disease, insisting that she had 'done nothing wrong'. She even repeated this in congressional testimony.

Understandably, this angered some homosexual Aids victims, as her comment implied they *had* done something wrong – and were being justly punished for it. This has been a popular stance among fundamentalists and may even have influenced some early mainstream indifference to Aids and its prey. Trying to make a play out of his interviews with Bergalis, Blessing included himself as playwright and a gay male in a rather lame colloquy. *Patient A* would have worked much better as a monologue by Bergalis, especially as played by Robin Morse for Signature.

Lake Street Extension, set in strife-ridden El Salvador, centres on an odd father who has sexually abused his son – driving him into the streets as a tormented hustler – but who has now seemingly reformed, seeking salvation in denial of the past and in dubious pieties. While realistic, the play may well be a political metaphor as well, another form of magic realism.

At the least serious level of gay sensibility this season were *Lypsinka! A Day in the Life*, *The Charles Busch Revue*, and two mini-lavish productions by the Ridiculous Theatrical Company,

Brother Truckers and *Linda*. John Epperson's Lypsinka, in a series of dazzling gowns and accessories, matching or clashing with elaborate settings, not only lip-synched to popular song recordings of great shows and films, but also brilliantly mimed taped ads, fashion tips, and telephone conversations from old broadcasts and movies, evoking the likes of Crawford and Stanwyck.

Unlike British panto dames, who are rude and crude enough so the audience will know they are male comics who aren't trying to pass for women, Epperson never suggests he is a male under all the makeup and high fashion. At the same time, in his comic hysteria he makes wonderful fun of feminine foibles with the woman he has created. Produced by the admirable New York Theatre Workshop before it went commercial at the Cherry Lane, this elegant cabaret made quite a change from *Vampire Lesbians*.

After the death from Aids of Charles Ludlam, the witty founder of the Theatre of the Ridiculous, his friend and heir, Everett Quinton, has been carrying on the tradition, but with productions much more chic than Ludlam's. Although Ludlam made Norma Desmond a famous personality at the Ridiculous, he often played equally mannered male roles. Quinton, on the other hand, is clearly in his element in drag and obviously enjoys appearing in an extensive, handsome wardrobe. That doesn't dull his comic edge, but it raises the hysteria-level on stage, wackily complementing the knockabout comedy of the rest of the cast.

Truckers may have owed something to *Blood Brothers*, but *Linda*'s antecedents are far more complex. Linda is a lesbian country and western singer reduced to operating a launderette in Dead Man's Gulch, Colorado. As in Aspen, there is a militant movement to stamp out deviant behaviour – nor do decent people want to see smutty shows. Unfortunately (recalling Auden and Kalmann's libretto for *Rake's Progress*), there is a noxious character – Armitage Shanks, played by Eureka – who has invented a machine to turn faeces into food. (This scatological humour must be a special taste: to me, it seemed repulsive in all aspects.)

Forces of 'good' are represented in *Linda* by Quinton as the Reverend Mrs. Charlotte Drum, a scheming religious fraud. In a dream-sequence, she's sent to Hell and condemned to the Lillian Hellman room, to hear the final scene from *The Children's Hour* over and over. (The breakthrough Broadway play, remember, in which the offending lesbian killed herself!) My programme jottings on *Linda*: excremental, incremental, detrimental.

Speaking of which, Joe Orton once told me he thought Americans were 'positively mental' about communism and homosexuality, and pro-posed a Gallup Poll question: 'Which would you rather have your son grow up to be, a commie or a queer?' He was certain that, much as the Red Menace was feared, a socialist at home would be thought preferable to a deviant – even in the closet. Now the Red Threat has gone – China doesn't seem to count: the Russians looked like *us* – that leaves hate-mongers only one broadly exposed target. Too bad Orton isn't around to deal with that.

Failing Orton, there were plenty of other British writers on view in the 1992-93 season. Simon Gray's *Holy Terror* extended the misanthropy one has come to expect of this playwright, thanks to a strong performance by Daniel Gerroll as the thoroughly dislikable Mark Melon, without making its circumstances seem believable – especially the putative lecture at the Cheltenham Women's Institute.

Despising people in general – or even oneself in particular – may be a powerful force in delineating character with killing insights, but it can also prove fatal to audiences. Hugh Whitemore's *The Best of Friends* – another letter-play – presented pleasant characters, GBS being well past his prime, but generated no real excitement or interest, despite Roy Dotrice as Shaw and Diana Douglas as Dame Laurentia.

Frank McGuinness's *Someone Who'll Watch Over Me* won accolades for Stephen Rea (to match those he'd won in *The Crying Game*) playing a hostage 'somewhere in the Middle East'. The drama seemed contrived, as if determined to exploit recent headlines, Terry Waite, *et al.* Alec McCowen and James McDaniel were also praised by critics. How could a reviewer criticize such prisoners – unless, of course, he also began to feel like a hostage in the theatre?

When Willy Russell's *Blood Brothers* opened on Broadway – more elaborately done than in London – the improbabilities of this tale of twin boys, separated in infancy, one to grow up poor and criminal, the other well-off and law-abiding, seemed even more unlikely than in the West End production. British – or is it English? – class distinctions and conflicts among people of roughly the same ethnic group remain a puzzle to many American theatregoers, though they've had a thorough course in such matters from John Osborne onwards. Nor were matters helped by having a cast of grown-ups play kiddies and teenagers for much of the evening. But Stephanie Lawrence and Con O'Neil of the London cast did win critical approval, though some tired rapidly of reprises of 'Marilyn Monroe'.

One of the most impressive imports from Britain was Caryl Churchill's *Mad Forest*, restaged for the Manhattan Theatre Club by Mark Wing-Davey, who went on to California's Berkeley Rep to do it in a different setting. Romania now is of course not Bosnia (more like an incipient Serbia), but the ironies of survival under malign tyranny were not lost on audiences. Marina Drahici's sets and costumes lent a powerful visual support to the starkness of the drama.

Churchill was also smartly celebrated by the New York Theatre Workshop in its new East Village home across from La Mama ETC. But *Traps*, as directed by Lisa Peterson, seemed trapped in a 'seventies hippie sensibility. *Owners*, strongly staged by Mark Wing-Davey in a remarkably post-postmodernist translucent plastic set, was truly terrifying, thanks in large part to a wonderful cast which included John Curless, Robert Stanton, J. Smith-Cameron, Lynn Hawley, and Tim Hopper.

The Irish Repertory Theatre staged Thomas Kilroy's *The Madame MacAdam Travelling Theatre* respectably at Actor's Playhouse. T. S. Eliot came vividly to life in an East Side church hall in Michael Hastings's *Tom and Viv*, courtesy of Prufrock Productions. And the American Jewish Theatre offered Ronald Harwood's painful tale of Jewish expatriates in South Africa, *Another Time*, with Malcolm McDowell, Marian Seldes, and Joan Copeland (sister of Arthur Miller and an admirable actress).

Janet Hayes Walker's York Theatre, which specializes in musicals old and new, presented a stylish staging of Sheridan Morley's *Noel and Gertie*, but Michael Zaslow and Jane Summer-hays, though attractive in their own rights, were nothing like the real thing. Not far from Broadway, at Philadelphia's venerable Walnut Street Theatre, an imaginative production of Alan Ayckbourn's *Henceforward* followed immediately on the heels of *The Old Devils*, Robin Hawdon's laboured version of Kingsley Amis's novel about the Man Who Knew Dylan Thomas. This was staged by Wales' own Toby Robertson, with sets by Franco Colavecchia.

Musicals remain the New Yorker's genre of choice. Gerard Alessandrini's *Forbidden Broadway*, now in a 1993 edition, couldn't survive without them. But with so few new entries, old musical parodies and hoary performer spoofs have to be endlessly recycled. Fresh meat for Alessandrini's satiric singing lions was readily provided by Neil Simon's *The Goodbye Girl*, a dismal remake of the film, with routine melodies by Marvin Hamlisch, pedestrian lyrics by David Zippel, and Martin Short in a comic frenzy to keep the audience's interest and affection. Bernadette Peters seemed lovely but listless. One didn't care if she kept the apartment or won the man, its legal tenant.

Jelly's Last Jam, a dancing fiction about Jelly Roll Morton and his music which opened late last season, continued a strong draw, staged like *Angels in America* by George C. Wolfe. *Ain't Broadway Grand*, 'A Brand New 1948 Musical Comedy', with songs by Mitch Leigh and Lee Adams, wasn't all that new, though previously

The Ridiculous Theatrical Company's production of *Linda*, featuring Everett Quinton (left) as 'a lesbian launderette proprietress country-western diva who struggles against sadistic censors with soap, suds, and song'. Photo: Paula Court.

unproduced on Broadway. Producer Mike Todd tries to be serious about musicals, but when his Martha Graham dances and social comment bombs in Boston, in desperation he saves the show with old burlesque comic Bobby Clark – he of the eyeglasses outlined on his face in mascara – and bevies of curvaceous cuties in elaborate but scanty costumes. All this was based on an actual Todd show, *As the Girls Go*, if that matters. Even The Who's *Tommy* isn't so new, but *this* material seemed ancient, and soon closed, despite a million dollars in sequins and boas.

From Spain, *Gypsy Passion*, a lame and lamentable flamenco evening, came briefly to

Broadway. Even swifter was the demise of *Tango Pasión*, choreographed by Hector Zaraspe and flown directly from Buenos Aires by United Airlines – as the programme prominently noted. *The Song of Jacob Zulu*, which lasted only slightly longer, was more complicated. Critics and audiences loved the songs of Ladysmith Black Mambazo, but the story of a young black who has killed people in a terrorist bombing – for principles which neither he nor the playwright could well articulate – fell on deaf ears so soon after the disastrous bombing of the World Trade Center.

Fool Moon featured old routines of two talented mimes, Bill Irwin and David Shiner, spelled by funky songs from the Red Clay Ramblers. Audiences adored it. In Greenwich Village, *Hello Muddah, Hello Fadduh!* revived the comic songs of Alan Sherman, a major talent in the 1960s, with albums such as 'My Son, the Folksinger', which sold over a million. Stephanie Mills, the original Dorothy, returned to Broadway in a revival of *The Wiz*, this time at the Beacon, thirty blocks further up town: but she still had the same youthful dynamism she had almost twenty years ago. Westside off-Broadway, Mark Nutter's 'musical . . . sort of', *Wild Men!*, made broad fun of the 'men's movement', and of Getting In Touch With Your Adult Child. It was notable for the likable clowning of George Wendt, of the now defunct TV series, *Cheers*.

Musical fever infected institutional theatres as well, some obviously hoping for a commercial transfer. Unfortunately, even with dances by Pat Birch, the Circle-in-the-Square's leaden *Anna Karenina* didn't work. It also lost so much that the rest of the season was crippled. At Lincoln Center's Vivian Beaumont, André Bishop, fresh from successful musical transfers at Playwright's Horizons, tried to repeat the Beaumont's recent success in reviving *Anything Goes*, but *My Favorite Year* didn't prove a favourite with critics or audiences. Don Scardinio, his Horizons successor, had better luck with Eric Overmyer, author of *On the Verge*, and his provocative imaginings in *The Heliotrope Bouquet by Scot Joplin and Louis Chauvin*, about an abandoned, dying Chauvin in a Chicago opium den, harried by Joplin to fulfil his musical promise.

The Manhattan Theatre Club brought Julie Andrews back – if not to Broadway, at least to City Center – in *Sondheim: Putting It Together*. Sondheim and Julia McKenzie devised this charmer, in which playwright Christopher Durang proved an admirable comic foil, though no threat to Stephen Collins or Michael Rupert on vocals. The York Theatre provided a prizewinning revival of *Carnival*, as well as a curiously coy *Six Wives*, with Steve Barton as Henry VIII and Tovah Feldshuh and Kim Crosby as all six spouses. Joe Masteroff, who did the book for *She*

Loves Me and *Cabaret*, provided both book and lyrics, but Edward Thomas's score didn't soar.

At the close of the season, the Roundabout Theatre launched a splendid revival on Broadway of *She Loves Me*, with songs by Jerry Bock and Sheldon Harnick. Tony Walton achieved a rich Budapest atmosphere on a low budget, thanks to a revolving stage, with Boyd Gaines and Judy Kuhn as a most attractive pair of lovers, both vocally and visually. Scott Ellis directed with verve.

Theda Bara and the Frontier Rabbi, at the Jewish Repertory Theatre, was ingeniously designed and charmingly acted and sung. Its conceit is that a young rabbi in Hollywood wants to make his mark, to honour his revered rabbi father. Denouncing sex on the cinema screen is his opening, but he falls in love with Bara when he sees her in action. Fortuitously, his sister becomes Bara's make-up girl, and Bara turns out to be a nice Jewish girl, less aggressive than Sis. Jeff Hochhauser's book and lyrics, with Bob Johnston also on lyrics and score, made this a delight.

More ambitious, and also far more problematic, was Circle Rep's *Orpheus in Love*, a musical spin-off of the old legend and classical opera. At the Public Theatre, Arthur Kopit's elegant and riveting *Wings*, which got the musical treatment from Jefrey Lunden, would have fared better with an operatic setting – or, even better left as it was, a haunting play about amnesia. Someone forgot this.

Marc Blitzstein's *Juno*, which Siobhan McKenna had long wanted to do, was revived by the Vinyard Theatre. In a wooden-beamed unit-set, Sean O'Casey's characters scampered about being very, very Irish, with Anita Gillette striving as Juno. What Blitzstein did, however, was to force O'Casey's plot and people into the Rodgers and Hammerstein Broadway format, with ballads, waltzes, and comic songs galore. The many musical forms on display did not serve the characters or their emotions well.

More successful was the City Opera's major revival of Blitzstein's *Regina*, based on Lillian Hellman's *The Little Foxes*. This was also created for Broadway, so there are similar showbiz musical touches which seem a bit alien to the plot, though perhaps justified in terms of the Southern milieu. Leigh Munro was a commanding Regina. Quite a different treat was City Opera's spacious revival of *110 in the Shade*, N. Richard Nash's *The Rainmaker*, with music by Harvey Schmidt and lyrics by Tom Jones. Karen Ziemba was a wonderful Lizzie, transformed from a plain girl into a beauty by an act of faith and love, and Brian Sutherland a big-voiced, handsome, athletic Starbuck. Scott Ellis staged, with brilliant choreography by Susan Stroman of *Crazy for You*.

In May 1993, the American (read New York) League of Theatres launched 'Broadway Celebrates'. The ostensible reason for this year-long festival was the centenary of the American Theatre – the first theatre on 42nd Street, though centred on Eighth Avenue rather than Broadway. Once huge and handsome, it's now long vanished, its site a vast parking lot. After long struggles, most of the remaining historic playhouses on that 'Theatre Block' are now closed, and under the wing of the 42nd Street Redevelopment Corporation, which has neither the funds to restore and operate the theatres – income from four unbuilt skyscrapers on Times Square was to have made that possible – nor viable ideas about productions which might fill these big houses.

For that matter, the three major powers which own and operate most Broadway theatres, the Shuberts, the Nederlanders, and Jujamcyn, have dificulty finding 'product', with a number of handsome theatres now dark. The Nederlander was aglow for a very short time with *Solitary Confinement* by Rupert Holmes, with Stacy Keach the sole performer in a wild super-TV fantasy of a Howard Hughes type bunkered in an electronic sky-suite. Aside from shows generated by institutional theatres, that sums up Broadway last season.

Curiously, the major owners, used to high stakes and large-volume business, have no interest in off-Broadway houses, which are limited to 299 seats. Off-Broadway non-institutional offerings included *CBS Live,* which included old episodes from *The Honeymooners* and *I Love Lucy; Avenu [sic] Boys,* which featured three white Brooklyn toughs and their girls – one in love with a black girl, one secretly fascinated with gay bars; and *Wrong Turn at Lungfish,* in which George C. Scott was a dying old misanthrope, educating Jami Gertz as his Rita in what looked like a TV sit-com pilot.

The most provocative off-Broadway commercial entry was David Mamet's *Oleanna,* with W. H. Macy as a young professor on the brink of tenure, destroyed by the politically correct malice of a seemingly dim, inept student, played by Mrs. David Mamet, Rebecca Pidgeon. With sexual harassment, notably on campuses, much in the news, this was timely but suffered from contrivance and from both characters sounding like Mamet.

Among the institutions, Circle Rep completed its season with John Robin Baitz's *Three Hotels,* a *tour de force* in three monologues – two by Ron Rifkin and one by Christine Lahti – unmasking unscrupulous American marketing methods of dangerous products in Africa, as well as stripping its characters bare. Circle also unwisely moved Lanford Wilson's *Redwood Curtain* to Broadway, where this improbable fiction was distinguished largely by John Lee Beatty's remarkable revolving Redwood forest.

Among a number of good shows at the Manhattan Theatre Club were *Pretty Fire,* a one-person childhood memoir by Charlayne Woodard, and Catherine Butterfield's fable of female bonding, *Joined at the Head.* Unfortunately, Arthur Miller's *The Last Yankee* was only about two baffled husbands with wives in a mental home. With titanic events in the world at large, where was the titan of *Death of a Salesman?*

Lee Blessing is not yet a titan, but he is the only American playwright who seems concerned with major issues. In addition to his *Patient A* and *Lake Street Extension,* Signature Theatre also gave us his *Fortinbras,* after the manner of Stoppard but also possibly an allegory of the Gulf War, and *Two Rooms* – a Beirut hostage drama more complex and compelling than Broadway's *Someone Who'll Watch over Me.* Last season, Signature presented only plays by Romulus Linney. Next season, Blessing will be followed by Edward Albee. An interesting production concept – deep immersion in one writer's recent work – admirably realized.

On non-commercial Broadway, Tony Randall's National Actors Theatre against the odds mounted a second season, this time at the historic Lyceum. *The Seagull* was a disaster, thanks to the miscasting of TV's Tyne Daly as Arkadina and director Marshall Mason's inattention to detail. Woody Allen's side-kick, Tony Roberts, was the most believable in the cast, as Dr. Dorn. Unbelievable. *Saint Joan,* with Maryann Plunkett a workaday Maid, saved the season, which finished limply with *Three Men on a Horse,* already too frequently revived, in which an ageing Randall played the youthful hero.

Also now on Broadway – and therefore eligible for Tony Awards – the Roundabout programmed revivals of George Kelly's *The Show-Off,* Shaw's *Candida,* and O'Neill's *Anna Christie.* The first had a nice 'twenties atmosphere, but the second seemed very un-Shavian, while the third – an awkward, embarrassing, dated drama – was welcomed by critics and audiences as the early salvation of the season, thanks to the sexual sparks set off by Natasha Richardson as Anna and Liam Neeson as Mat Burke.

Very near Broadway in tiny theatres, the Lambs offered a moving revival of Horton Foote's *The Roads to Home.* Among a number of ventures, Playwrights Horizons staged *On the Bum,* a quixotic vision of the Great Depression, replete with rail-hopping hoboes, small-town meanness, and quasi-WPA projects. Somnolent most of the season for lack of funds and ideas, the American Place Theatre presented an indictment of the man who embodied Hollywood's politically incorrect image of black males for many years, the one-man show *The Confessions of Stepin Fetchit.* New York's influential African-American congressman Charles Rangel took part in a post-performance discussion. His wife disagreed with him.

Beyond Broadway, the Pearl Theatre made Oliver Goldsmith's awkward *The Good Natur'd Man* most enjoyable. And its *Widowers' Houses* – awkward in a different way – was better Shaw than the Roundabout's. The excellent Atlantic Theatre, with David Mamet as a guiding light, staged Gary Richards's *The Root*, a terrifyingly real and violent drama about a crooked cop and a chop-shop where stolen cars are dismembered.

The Jewish Repertory Theatre made a mistake with its adaptation of Sholem Asch's *God of Vengeance*. As the Jewish brothel-keeper's pure daughter runs off to become a whore, one had the sensation of reliving hammy Yiddish melodramas on Second Avenue in the late nineteenth century. No relation, the American Jewish Theatre offered *Born Guilty*, Ari Roth's dramatization of Peter Sichrovsky's book of conversations with Germans about the Nazi era. Jack Gelber – many years ago author of *The Connection* – directed an excellent cast with vigour. And at the Classic Stage Company, in addition to *Scapin* an addled Canadian comedy, *Goodnight Desdemona (Goood Morning Juliet)*, featured Cherry Jones as a kooky academic with an odder even than usual interpretation of Shakespeare's secrets.

Despite a shortage of money, La Mama was able to offer a number of domestic and foreign experiments, the latter subsidized by admiring culture ministries. Among these were *Expropriados*, from Spain's Arena Teatro; Richard Schechner's novel and scatalogical *Faust Gastronome* – hero as chef rather than alchemist; *Ghosts Live from Galilee*, the 'Scottsboro Boys Blues Opera'; *500 Years: a Fax from Denise Stoklos to Christopher Columbus* – wildly funny and athletic performance art; *Underground*, Theodora Skiptares' novel vision of people who live and work beneath the earth; Ping Chong's lovely *Deshima*; the far, far-out *Every Day Newt Burman (The Trilogy of Cyclic Existence)*; and an excellent revival of Christopher Hampton's *Tales from Hollywood*. After three decades of avant-garde enrichment in New York, La Mama's founder, Ellen Stewart, was finally honoured in June 1993 by the Municipal Art Society.

No such honour was in store for the Public Theatre's artistic director, Joanne Akalaitis, Joseph Papp's personal choice as his successor. Fresh from critical raves and boos for her deconstructionist vision of *Woyzeck*, she went to a board meeting only to be summarily fired. She was rapidly replaced by George C. Wolfe (of *Angels* and *Jelly's Last Jam*), who has had several successes at the Public. But Wolfe, like Akalaitis, is primarily a director, not a producer, which is what the Public now sorely needs. Kevin Kline is to shape Shakespeare offerings.

Akalaitis was variously charged with having too many of the Public's theatres dark too often, with programming too many monologues – Marga Gomez' *Memory Tricks* and Ann Magnuson's *You Could Be Home Now* were typical, interesting but uninspiring; and with lavishing too much time and money on her own productions. Although she didn't direct the expensively devastated production of Steve Tesich's *On the Open Road* – Mother Courage cloned with Didi and Gogo – some of the complaints were justified. What was not was the way in which the board dealt with Akalaitis, a respected if oddly inspired director.

She shouldn't have been put in the position of a producer in the first place: she had neither the inclination nor the experience. In any case, the board should have retained her as a staff director. Such behaviour is to be expected on Broadway, but not in the institutional theatre. Still, Papp himself – an awkward director who none the less preferred that role to being a producer – on occasion gave short shrift to directors in mid-production so he could take over and 'save the show'. Maybe the Public is haunted by Papp's Curse?

Across the East River in Brooklyn, the lone outpost of High Culture continued to be BAM, the Brooklyn Academy of Music. Neither funding cuts nor audience fears of the borough's mean streets after dark could deter its chief, Harvey Lichtenstein, from mounting a leanly impressive season. Among the notable productions were a revival of Robert Wilson's *Einstein on the Beach*; the Théâtre du Soleil's *Les Atrides*; the Netherlands Opera's *The Return of Ulysses*; *Frida*, the story of Frida Kahlo; Mark Morris's art deco revision of *The Nutcracker* as *The Hard Nut*; and Ingmar Bergman's strong Swedish stagings of Ibsen's *Peer Gynt* and Mishima's *Madame de Sade*, from Stockholm's Royal Dramatic Theatre.

As the nature of theatre production in New York – and across the nation – gradually changes, institutions are filling the void left by commercial producers. This means, at least in New York, shorter runs in much smaller theatres. But it does not mean a marked falling-off in productions – just that more of them are semi-professional or verging on amateur and offered in venues remote from the Great White – or was that Gay? – Way.

NTQ Book Reviews

edited by Viv Gardner

Theatre History to 1900

Phyllis Rackin
Stages of History:
Shakespeare's English Chronicles
London: Routledge, 1991. 256 p. £14.99.
ISBN 0-415-05839-2.

This book is potentially much bigger than a mere study of Shakespeare's history plays. It describes Renaissance England's attitude to and uses of history: tensions between providentialist and more materialist, 'Machiavellian' explanations of historical causality; feelings about history shaped by senses of its present relevance and its irrecoverable loss; discourses of official history and genealogy shaped to distort and silence the voices of women and lower-class people.

Usefully ranging across Renaissance and modern historiography, it also suggestively conjectures about how an audience is worked on by different senses of time or shifts between textures of speech. It is clearly written, for a student reader, though rather repetitive, and the simplicity sometimes becomes simplistic or schematic, tending for example to overstress the (currently trendy) concept of subversive theatricality. The general arguments are interesting: they could have been much more so if Shakespeare's work had not been segregated from contemporary drama.

SIMON SHEPHERD

Christopher Cairns, ed.
Three Renaissance Comedies
Lewiston; Queenston; Lampeter: Edwin Mellen Press, 1991. 353 p. £39.95.
ISBN 0-7734-9450-2.

James Fisher
The Theatre of Yesterday and Tomorrow:
Commedia dell'Arte on the Modern Stage
Lewiston; Queenston; Lampeter: Edwin Mellen Press, 1992. 408 p. £49.95
ISBN 0-7734-9529-0.

Mention of Italian Renaissance comedy probably conjures up in most readers' minds a vision of the vigorously professional *commedia dell'arte*, with its stock characters, improvised playing, and farcical *lazzi*: indeed, as James Fisher's study testifies, there have been few periods since the sixteenth century in which the *commedia* tradition and its imaginative reinterpretations have not been active. The so-called *commedia erudita* which helped to shape it can easily be dismissed as a rather dull academic forerunner whose trite and repetitive subject matter is redeemed only by Machiavelli's *La Mandragola* and the dazzling *intermedi* which all too often overshadowed the plays which provided their occasion.

Richard Andrews's *Scripts and Scenarios: the Performance of Comedy in Renaissance Italy* (Cambridge, 1993), which looks likely to become a standard work on its subject, does much to redress the balance for English readers by bringing out the diversity and theatrical vitality of the best of the scripted comedies written in sixteenth century Italy; the promised series published by the Edwin Mellen Press under the general editorship of Christopher Cairns should also make a useful contribution by rendering the plays more accessible to those students whose appetites have perhaps been whetted by *Scripts and Scenarios*. His first volume, which contains Ariosto's *Lena*, Ruzante's *Posh Talk* (*La Moscheta*), and Aretino's *Talanta* has on the whole achieved the task of providing accessible translations with adequate accompanying commentary.

Translating sixteenth-century Italian comedies can be uphill work: and Ruzante, operating in 'a complex and fluid multilingual context', baffles even the Italians. Each of the translators has negotiated his own path between the need for readable, stageworthy texts and fidelity to the original. The editor notes that contributors to the series are 'left entirely free to choose the style of their translation and the breadth and scope of the introduction', and whether by accident or design, this *laissez faire* policy has paid off in the first volume, although perhaps future additions to the series would benefit if all the translations had succinct endnotes like those supplied for *Posh Talk*.

C. P. Brand's introduction to Ariosto's comedy provides a broad introduction to the scope of early *commedia erudita* and shows how Ariosto, while bowing to classical precedent, increasingly coloured his comedies with local realism; Ronnie Ferguson's introduction to Angelo Beolco (Ruzante), the most complex and fascinating of all the Italian dramatists of the period ('constantly anti-urban and anti-intellectual, he was himself a type of urban intellectual') is essential reading for those with no access to Italian; and Cairns's own introduction to Aretino's rambling comedy focuses on its moral and intellectual background while showing how it foreshadows the nascent *commedia dell'arte* in some of its characters and techniques.

The subsequent influence of *commedia dell'arte*, paying no respect to international frontiers or even artistic genres, is so widespread that it is perhaps one of those subjects which justifies a collection of essays by different specialists, as in the recently published *Studies in the Commedia dell'Arte*, edited by David George and Christopher Gossip (Cardiff: University of Wales Press, 1993). Certainly James Fisher's study covers much of its material fairly superficially, coming to life only in those areas of twentieth-century theatre in which the author has a more particular interest. And to end on a querulous note, I hope that the poor standard of proof-reading will be addressed in future volumes issuing from the Edwin Mellen Press.

MICHAEL ANDERSON

Twentieth-Century Theatre

Patrick Miles, ed.
Chekhov on the British Stage
Cambridge: Cambridge University Press, 1993. 258 p. £30.00, $59.95.
ISBN 0-521-38467-2.

This edited volume is the first to examine the 'reading' of Chekhov in production, criticism, and translation on the British stage across a wide range of theatre practices. Most articles confirm Patrick Miles's introductory view that Chekhov has acquired a place next to Shakespeare on the British stage: many explore the cultural implications as well as the causes of this phenomenon.

Some trace its history – in the various attempts to bring the Moscow Art Theatre to England prior to 1914; the cultural confrontation between British and Russian views of Chekhov (and of Stanislavsky) when the MKhAT did tour in 1958, 1964, and 1970; Komisarjevsky's 'romantic lovers' inflection of *The Three Sisters*, which prepared the way for Chekhov's acceptance in the British theatrical canon; the shift from the pre-1914 'dramatic reformer' emphasis of the avant-garde, which led to a comparative lack of interest in Chekhov, to the later stylistic challenges (Mike Alfreds), ideological challenges (Richard Eyre, Trevor Griffiths), and linguistically-inspired 'rules of conversation' interpretations (Jonathan Miller).

Other contributions focus directly on the problems of cultural transformation and transcodification – among actors, translators, directors, designers, and critics, as well as between changing historical national cultures (Russian,

English, and Welsh). Very clearly written, and well edited, this book will appeal to all who are professionally, intellectually, or emotionally involved with Chekhov.

JOHN TULLOCH

Hersh Zeifman and Cynthia Zimmerman, eds.
Contemporary British Drama, 1970-1990
Basingstoke; London: Macmillan, 1993. 348p. £40.
ISBN 0-333-49114-9.

This collection of essays, selected from twenty years of *Modern Drama*, focuses upon writers regarded as significant by 'the general critical consensus' (Introduction). The essays chosen employ a variety of critical methodologies, and Pinter, Shaffer, Bond, and Stoppard get multiple treatments while Ayckbourn, Hampton, Storey, Gray, Griffiths, Churchill, and Brenton receive just one essay apiece.

As a kind of 'second wave' supplement, this book makes some excellent essays more accessible and will be a very useful addition to library stocks on post-war British theatre. Coverage of the period is problematical, however: it is skewed towards the 1970s, and the close focus on individual writers tends to erase some features of recent theatre history. The fact that there is only one woman in the elite group, for example, is remarkable. The editors note that this is partly a result of what has been submitted to the magazine, but although both C. W. E. Bigsby and Richard Johnstone address broader issues (socialist theatre, television drama) the selection is ultimately rather conservative.

DEREK PAGET

Trevor R. Griffiths and Margaret Llewellyn-Jones, eds.
British and Irish Women Dramatists since 1958: a Critical Handbook
Buckingham: Open University Press, 1993. 193 p. £37.50 (hbk), £12.99 (pbk).
ISBN 0-335-09603-4 (hbk), 0-335-09602-6 (pbk).

This book includes a range of essays in the broad area of women's theatres. The title is a little misleading, as only one essay on Irish theatre is included, and this is not so much a 'critical handbook' as an introduction to trends and developments in the field. It devotes more space to description than analysis, and does not engage (or claim to engage) in any detail with either feminist theory or performance theory, nor does it outline its methodology for analyzing the trends described.

But what the book does do is important: it fills some significant gaps in the published literature, and will in this sense be most valuable to students and those interested in recent social and theatre history. Several of the essays stand out, notably Margaret Llewellyn-Jones's on 'Women Dramatists in Wales', Anna McCullan's piece on 'Irish Women Playwrights since 1958', and Susan Treisman's on 'Women's Discourse on the Scottish Stage'. The book would suit readers with a broad interest in women's writing and the theatre, or with a special interest in the regional representation of women in the arts.

LIZBETH GOODMAN

M. Buning, S. Houppermans, and D. de Ruyter, eds.
Samuel Beckett Today / Aujourd'hui:
Vol. 1, Samuel Beckett 1970-1989
Amsterdam: Editions Rodopi, 1992.
ISBN 90-5183-347-4.

Eoin O'Brien
The Beckett Country
Dublin: Black Cat Press; London: Faber and Faber, 1986. 426 p. £40.00.
ISBN 0-571-04667-8.

Samuel Beckett Today is a collection of essays which aims to focus on Beckett's bilingualism. Some articles are in French and some in English (not translations), arranged by genre: fiction, poetry, drama, and film. The most useful article on the drama is written in French – a well-informed essay by Matthijs Engleberts which examines with rigour and clarity Beckett's use of narrative in the later plays. Paul Smith and Nic van der Toorn address (in French) the role of didascalies in Beckett's plays as texts to be read, and Tjebbe Westendorp considers Jonathan Kalb's assessment of Beckett's dramatic practice.

Cobi Bordewijk's article, 'The Integrity of the Playtext: Disputed Performances of *Waiting for Godot*', though sometimes reductive in its arguments, includes useful material on productions opposed by Beckett, including those by George Tabori. I would also recommend an essay by Leslie Hill on mourning in the fiction, using the concepts of introjection and incorporation, which could be applied to dramatic texts such as *Footfalls* and *Ohio Impromptu*. The volume is worth consulting, particularly for francophones, and offers a welcome outlet for a European perspective on Beckett.

The publication of *The Beckett Country* was designed to coincide with Beckett's eightieth year. Glossily produced, and containing striking black and white photographs by David Davison, the book is primarily an exploration and celebration of the place of Ireland, and particularly, of Dublin and the surrounding land and seascapes, in the life and work of Samuel Beckett. The foreword by J. R. Knowlson and the author's introduction raise pertinent questions about Beckett's creative use of his memories of specific

places, figures, and incidents from his life in Ireland, although, on the whole, the author has chosen to leave critical interpretation of the material to the reader, juxtaposing images or descriptions with Beckett's own texts.

These, however, are largely drawn from the fiction, poetry, or criticism, and for students or researchers specifically interested in Beckett's drama or in questions of dramatic form, the book contains little directly relevant material. *The Beckett Country* therefore invites rather than provides a re-interpretation of Beckett's texts in an Irish context, which it explores mainly in terms of people and places, with consideration, via the National Gallery, of an artistic context, and some brief references to Shaw, Yeats, Synge, and O'Casey.

ANNA MCMULLAN

Sidney Homan
Pinter's Odd Man Out:
Staging and Filming *Old Times*
Lewisburg: Bucknell University Press, 1993.
£26.00.
ISBN 0-8387-5238-1.

Pinter's Odd Man Out is not just about the staging and filming of *Old Times*, it is also a ruminative discussion of Pinter's work overall. The first chapter, for instance, gives a brief history of the play and of how it has been critically received, and the second offers an analysis of dominant generic features which run through much of Pinter's playwriting and which are later applied to *Old Times*. The bulk of Homan's book, however, is dedicated to his own specific producions.

The paradox is that this book is both too broad and too specific. The more wide-ranging opening chapters canter rather inelegantly through several fields – from cataloguing what virtually every critic said about *Old Times* when it was premiered to an exhaustive account of such Pinteresque obsessions as rooms, the outside, language, and gender relations. Although most of these observations are sound if rather predictable, the fundamental problem with making so many generalizations is that sometimes they don't stand up to specific scrutiny.

Homan's territory is vast, and after this initial charge a reader necessarily pauses for breath. Enter *Old Times*. The production process is laid out before us in a faultlessly systematic way, beginning with the contextualization of *Old Times* within the parameters of the previous discussions, and proceeeding to an analysis of particular practical aspects such as blocking, lighting, the set, and the rehearsal process. But without any accompanying visual material to offer assistance, it is difficult to engage with such specific and subjective material.

This begs the question of who Homan envisaged his readership to be – beyond those directly involved with his productions of *Old Times,* or those who are themselves putting on the play. His reasons for shifting the camera, for example, and discussions of positions in the studio are no doubt valid, but difficult to agree or to dispute without recourse to the production itself.

Homan concludes with a hardly necessary summing up in which he attests that the book has been about the 'interaction among playwright, director, actor, and character'. The exclusion of the audience is telling, and goes some way towards explaining why reading *Pinter's Odd Man Out* felt rather like sneaking a peek at someone's diary and realizing it's not as interesting as you had hoped.

STELLA BRUZZI

David L. Hirst
Giorgio Strehler
Cambridge University Press, 1993. 140 p.
£32.50, $54.95.
ISBN 0-521-30768-6.

This first significant study in English of the innovative theatrical artistry of Italy's Giorgio Strehler is a most welcome and valuable addition to the CUP 'Directors in Perspective' series. Strehler, who stepped onto the international stage in the late 1940s with a vividly fantastic revival (and reconstruction) of Goldoni's *Arlecchino, the Servant of Two Masters* restored Goldoni's credentials as a dramatist – and made Strehler's Piccolo Teatro di Milano (and, later, his Paris-based Théâtre de l'Europe) an influential forerunner of the contemporary trend towards imaginative revaluations of dramatic classics (particularly neglected works) not only of the Italian canon, but also of European and American plays and operas.

Hirst's slim but well-written and evocative text wisely organizes itself around the major aspects of Strehler's prolific career. He laces his explications with ample quotes from Strehler himself – an articulate spokesman for his own work. Following two introductory chapters on the major factors that typify Strehler's style (interest in *commedia dell'arte* traditions and techniques, lyrical realism, incorporation of elements from epic theatre and naturalism), Hirst presents individual chapters assessing Strehler's direction and unique visions of three dramatists whose plays obviously fascinate Strehler and inform his productions of other works: Goldoni ('right to the bitter end he followed his destiny, his comic genius, his wandering genius, his genius for life. Always watching and evaluating; fascinated, trying to understand: as much as he could, and

more'); Shakespeare ('I have to approach Shakespeare with great caution and care. Get under the surface of the text, but never go against it or abuse it'); and Brecht ('The work of demystification we are pursuing in capitalist countries is the direct result of epic theatre and particularly of Brecht's theatre. . . . It isn't enough to show how the world is changing; you must also show what mankind can and must do to change the world').

A final chapter examines Strehler's ventures into opera, particularly the works of Verdi ('What is really needed is a proper musical education for a new public; instead of that phoney Italian passion for opera: an elitist ideal based on snobbery and ignorance'). A complete list of productions from 1943 to 1991 is appended, along with a brief bibliography and seventeen black-and-white illustrations that at least go some distance to provide the reader with a sample of Strehler's unique visual interpretations. Hirst's persuasive synthesis of the diverse strands of Strehler's development and style presents ample evidence to support his respected and integral position in European theatre.

JAMES FISHER

Richard Fotheringham
Sport in Australian Drama
Cambridge University Press, 1992. 268 p. $AUS40.
ISBN 0-521-40156-9.

This unusual thematic approach to Australian theatre history has resulted in a coverage of sport and drama which spans two centuries. Loosely divided into sections exploring sporting drama as a genre, the relationship of sport to drama, and sport in literary drama, the historical analysis is fresh and informative beyond the lameness that the title suggests. At its centre is a cultural thesis arguing that ideas about mass entertainment, particularly the bifurcation between sport and drama in colonial Australia, need to be re-thought (they did after all share personnel, entrepreneurs, and publications).

The construction of theatre in a colonial society is the great strength of this history. This weakens in the later chapters concerning 'Sport in Australian Film' and the literary dramas of the twentieth century, where more audience analysis is required; and critical precision slips during the discussion of the ramifications of feminist theatre on sport as a theme in contemporary drama, for example. An original and fascinating history, this book is a useful introduction to the character of Australian theatre in general, and of significant relevance to Commonwealth scholars and melodrama specialists.

SUSAN PFISTERER-SMITH

Performance, Theory, General Studies

Alan Read
Theatre and Everyday Life:
an Ethics of Performance
London; New York: Routledge, 1993. 260 p. £35.00.
ISBN 0-415-06940- 8.

At a women's liberation movement conference in 1977 a woman got up and said 'I'm running a workshop on sex, I don't just want a load of theories, I want to know what people actually do.' (It became the most popular workshop of the conference!) This incident came to mind whilst reading *Theatre and Everyday Life*. Phrases like 'a space opens up between', 'in the margins of', or the 'trace', 'tract', 'feint of'. . . at first seemed suggestive but were ultimately a source of frustration because they don't relate to what theatre makers actually *do*.

The author makes all manner of metaphorical and analytical links between 'theatre' and biological functions, 'psychogeography', phenomenology, surrealism, the avant garde, and poststructuralist literary criticism, and declares a sympathy with the postmodern project. He also claims to be rooted in socialism, but a definition of what this means and its implications is not forthcoming. So we are provided with an eclectic range of analytical frameworks with little attention given to their application to actual theatre production.

The fundamental problem that runs throughout this book is the author's reluctance to provide specific material examples of what he is talking about. In the first part he begins by telling us something of a project set up by Dartington Hall College called the 'Rotherhithe Theatre Workshop'. However, because of his unwillingness to provide straightforward factual information the reader is made to struggle to piece together a picture of what actually happened. We learn at one point that the author is working on a factory line. Why? Was this a requirement of the project? Was this research? Did all the students do it? For how long? With what result? Was this done, for political (by whatever definition) reasons or for artistic reasons? So many questions emerge as a result of sheer frustration rather than stimulated by an account which could provoke further research.

The second half of the book, which uses the natural elements as its chapter headings, makes interesting reading. It is concerned to show the influence of biological and environmental phenomena on theatrical work. The introduction of fire regulations and the safety curtain, for example, removed danger from the audience but also deprived them of a potential elemental experience. The author further regrets the demise of a docklands vinegar factory – twentieth century society being marked by 'olfactory sanitization'. Yet he chooses to examine these findings in a theoretical context such as Derrida's critique of Artaud, the historiography of Michel de Certeau, or Humphrey Jennings and the Mass Observation movement, which by a process of association become linked with the particular element. How this relates to the ex-employees of the vinegar factory who are presumably concerned in some way with the 'lay theatre' of 'everyday life' referred to in earlier chapters is not made clear.

In book reviewing it is almost becoming a cliché to complain of an impenetrable style or obscurantism. What is more important is to understand the reasons why. This text is difficult because it does not elucidate the material basis of its enquiry and continually argues from one theoretical position to another without specific theatrical example. In one sense the sheer breadth of scholarship is impressive, but there are far too many fleeting references whose sources are not contextualised. Like the author, I am deeply concerned by the split between the theory and practice of theatre which is prevalent in both the theatre establishment and academic institutions: hence my frustration and disappointment with this work.

ANNA SEYMOUR

Shomit Mitter
Systems of Rehearsal
London; New York: Routledge: 1992. 179 p.
£35.00 (hbk), £9.99 (pbk).
ISBN 0-415-06783-9.

There is much in this book of value to both the student and the practitioner. There are detailed descriptions of rehearsal techniques and, more importantly, perceptive discussions of the aesthetic and ideological implications behind their use. Mitter's own reliance on a 'somatic' approach, by which an actor's creativity is awakened by physical enactment rather than by intellectual analysis, does nothing to detract from his admirably succinct and clear exposition of the practices and the theories of Stanislavsky, Brecht, and Grotowski, who although they are not the only 'theatrical giants' that he could have considered do represent three major strands of theatrical performance in the twentieth century.

By concentrating on the contradictory aspects of their techniques – Stanislavsky's use of the physical, Brecht's sense of the comic, and Grotowski's distrust of audiences – he opens up whole areas of appreciation that cast new light on the traditional evaluation of their work. However, his strategy of discussing each in turn with reference to the work of Peter Brook creates one major drawback. Despite the assertion at the start that Brook's eclecticism makes him seem to Mitter 'more a mimic than an innovator', and 'a singularly canny user of other people's ideas and techniques', the fact that each of his other subjects is presented as a quarry from which Brook has skilfully sculpted a number of very different works of art means that it is he who emerges as the giant, not as one perched on the giants' shoulders.

Perhaps Mitter is right to argue that – from Brook's own point of view – 'it was a virtue to cast around widely for styles', but if he had found a way of shifting Brook out of the foreground and into a wider perspective in order to compare him with the other 'more genuinely innovative' directors, this book would have better fulfilled its potential as one of the most lucid expositions of the mysteries of the rehearsal room presently available.

GEORGE TAYLOR

Erik Exe Christofferson, trans. Richard Fowler
The Actor's Way
London; New York: Routledge, 1993. 224 p.
£35.00 (hbk), £10.99 (pbk).
ISBN 0 415-08795-3 (hbk), 0 415-08796-1 (pbk).

Translated from the Danish, this is a riveting account of the work of Eugenio Barba's Odin Teatret, one of the most innovative and longest-lived countercultural theatre companies established in the experimental ferment of the 'sixties, and still dedicated to creating new varieties of performance. The book's format effectively intersperses a developmental history of the company (regrettably not exploring its vital longevity) and its productions with actor interviews about training practices and theoretical analysis. The attempt to theorize the actor's new way of being present in performance is the weakest point. Much more insightful are the montage juxtapositions of objective descriptions of the productions with the actors' own accounts from within, particularly of the build-up of their own apparitional incarnations, which take us to the very heart of the intensity of Odin performances.

The fascinating pictorial documentation is fundamental to communicating and understanding the energy of Odin's presence, although the original contained much more than is given here. Odin's work helped to establish and engages deeply with all the markers of contemporary performance – especially multiculturalism, cross-gendering, and intertheatricality – and this book is a key to unlocking its complexities. One of the questions I am asked most frequently by my directing students is how to break away from naturalistic, psychological modes of performance, and I welcome these valuable wanderings on that 'stork' of a quest.

ALAN PEARLMAN

Patsy Rodenburg
The Need for Words
London: Methuen, 1993. 266 p. £9.99.
ISBN 0-413-67500-9.

Readers could be forgiven for thinking that publishers had declared open season on voice technique for the stage, with recent books by Evangeline Machlin, J. Clifford Turner, and now Patsy Rodenburg. However, apart from Rodenburg's work, these were reissues and revisions of earlier texts: now, Methuen has had the courage to commission afresh. Rodenburg's earlier volume for Methuen, *The Right to Speak*, essentially dealt with the physicality of vocal work, offering a progressive range of exercises framed by basic principles and useful advice to inform the exercise programme itself.

Building on these ideas *The Need for Words* is structured in two parts. The first offers a critical analysis of the reasons for what Rodenburg sees as society's present cultural alienation from language. She explores the problems and barriers which she believes block us from experiencing the power of language so that 'much of our speaking energy is wasted', and argues an impassioned case for the centrality of oracy both in education and everyday life.

In pursuit of 'our natural right to speak', the second part of her book outlines a variety of exercises which encourage experimentation with language in order to develop an awareness of, essentially, how words work. This section is focused on connecting voice and text, and includes a range of text extracts around which exercises are grouped and contextualized.

Rodenburg writes from a wide-ranging base of experience with both conviction and clarity. Students, teachers, actors, and directors will find in her books a rich seam of ideas aimed at practically and creatively facilitating our reappraisal of the exactness of the relationship between sound and meaning. Student actors in particular could do no better than to take and personalize these ideas as a means of forming a bedrock for their own, individual voice development regime.

TONY GOODE